D0731706

Among Other Things

A selection of columns, feature articles and Photographs from the author's 57 years in the Weekly newspaper business.

By Paul Fugleberg

To Carole —
Best Wishes
Paul Fugleberg

Gull Printing, Polson, MT

Table of Contents

Table of Contents
(Continued)

Dedication

Lorin Jacobson
May 3, 1925 – March 25, 2008

What words come to mind when trying to define the term "role model?" I think of honest, kind, considerate, patient, humble, hard working, fair, even tempered, have a sense of humor, calm, willing to work quietly behind the scenes, a peace maker, encouraging others, the ability to listen, empathetic, interested in others, spiritual, and having an obvious love of family, friends and his community and nation.

Those are just a few of the attributes that come to mind when trying to define the life of Lorin Jacobson, who died unexpectedly March 25, 2008.

He was truly a man for all seasons. Above all, he was a family man who will be missed deeply by his wife Shirley, their sons Rod, Brad, Jim and Jeff, and grandchildren. He was a leader in his church, veterans' groups, the Polson-Flathead Historical Museum, the Sons of Norway, supporter of school activities and had coached Little League baseball teams.

I appreciated having him as partner in the Flathead Courier from 1963-1976 and the Ronan Pioneer from 1971-1976. There could have been no better a business partner than Lorin, as we navigated the sometimes narrow straits of a start-up, shoestring business operation.

He went on to own and operate the A&W Root Beer franchise and then to serve as Lake County Clerk and Recorder before retiring. The term retirement was a misnomer. Lorin continued his involvement in church, community and veterans activities, even raising a small flock of sheep for a few years, despite several health issues.

We'll always treasure his memory and we thank God for placing Lorin Jacobson in our lives.

Acknowledgments

Following my May 1, 2008, retirement, the decision to put the time, effort and expense into publishing this book was a difficult one to make. However, helping me to decide to go ahead were the encouragement and moral support of family members – sons Alan, Mark and Tom and daughters Ruth and Laurie, sister-in-law Roberta Erickson, my brother Norman Wright; former co-workers Jim Blow and Ethan Smith; and friends, the late Bill Barba, Neal and Karen Lewing, Carmine Mowbray, Dick Christopher, and many others, too numerous to list, and the many readers of my columns over the years. Thank you so much! Without your comments and nudging, I'd still be procrastinating.

Also appreciated are the folks at the Lake County Leader for continuing to run the articles on a scheduled basis. Thanks, too, to K.C. and Cindy Sorensen of PC Rescue for their help in updating my computer skills, to Jenna Cederberg and daughter-in-law Christine Fugleberg for scanning photos, and thanks to Dan O'Donnell, who designed the book cover, and Chip Kurzenbaum and Joyce Kackmann of Gull Printing for production efforts.

Introduction

57 years a writin'

Holy mackerel! I recently realized that I started writing newspaper columns 57 years ago. Sure doesn't seem that long. Started out with the civilian-owned weekly newspaper at Great Falls Air Force Base (now Malmstrom AFB) in 1952.

While serving as a Link Trainer instructor, I started writing *The Wonderin' GI* column. Looking back at some of those columns now, I can't help but cringe. Come to think of it, looking back at a lot of 'em I've written since then, I cringe with embarrassment, too.

Eventually, the editor of the base paper left the service – and I was transferred over to Information Services Office and was named editor. That's how I stumbled into a newspaper career after taking a semester of journalism in college and disliking it so much, that I switched to a history major.

With the mentoring of Great Falls Tribune state editor, the late Mike Deevy – who owned the base paper – and working with the local media on air base stories, I quickly came to enjoy the news business. After being discharged from the service in 1954, I spent a couple years at Roundup, Montana, with the *Record-Tribune* where the column became *Main Street Musings.* Then came 18 months with the *Sioux Valley News* in Canton, South Dakota, where the column heading *Among Other Things* was born.

After six months at Bishop, California, with the *Inyo Register* as news editor and writing features, it was onto Polson, Montana, where the present title, *Among Other Things,* continued.

Over the years the columns have covered a myriad of topics including feature type pieces with pictures; giving "done good" recognition items to citizens for their accomplishments; unusual occupations; a long standing "feud" with the late Doc Eggensperger of the *Sanders County Ledger;* interviews with notable citizens, actors, artists and authors; personal philosophizin'; travel and/or historical articles; ramblin' type pieces; some goofy, nonsensical items and many more that can't even be categorized.

There have been extremely painful columns to write, too – eulogies about my wife's death, the death of our infant son, Jimmy, and the passing of scores of friends and acquaintances who contributed so much to community and country.

All in all, it's been an interesting and rewarding career and I feel so lucky and thankful.

After completing the *Proud Heritage* book and the four booklets in the Touch of Montana series, I pondered the feasibility of writing another book or two of some of the more interesting people, places and things that the columns and illustrated features have covered. Many topics would be timeless. But I procrastinated.

I became bit by the book bug again when I started reading Mack McConnell's enjoyable book titled *Never Grab a Cockatiel.* McConnell is a veteran weekly reporter and editor who in recent years was editor and columnist for *Rural Montana Magazine.* The book is a collection of some of his *Writetrack* and *Off the Cuff* columns. They're fun reading. Mack, now retired, lives in St. Ignatius.

Anyway, I say, "Thank you, I think" to Mack for his book that motivated me to do this book which carries the *Among Other Things* column heading for its title. If you enjoy it, tell others

Shadows of Yesteryear

The Railroads

Last spike at Gold Creek

Events of lasting significance often occur in remote areas, far removed from centers of civilization. Such an event occurred August 22, 1883, at Gold Creek, Montana Territory.

It was there that the last spike was driven home to complete the Northern Pacific's transcontinental rail line from Lake Superior to Puget Sound.

The event was a pivotal point in the history of the Pacific Northwest. It set the stage for a new surge of settlement and development – bringing into production new farm and ranch lands through government homestead programs and sale of cheap railroad land.

As later branch lines were built, the railroad meant easier access to markets for farmers, ranchers, and miners. There'd be new towns and cities, new business opportunities, increased importance for Montana's rich resources. Within six years, Montana would attain statehood.

As usual, progress was not without its problems: The Indians were squeezed out of more lands and their way of life was further limited; the territory's natural resources were exploited to the advantage of out-of-territory interests; and colorful, often corrupt, political practices evolved.

The concept for a northern cross-country railroad had its roots back in the 1840s. In 1864, President Abraham Lincoln signed a bill chartering the Northern Pacific Railroad Company and authorizing it to construct the line. With the charter came a grant of some 47 million acres and authorization to issue $100 million in stock. But NP president Josiah Perham was prohibited from mortgaging the railroad or the land grant for issuance of construction bonds.

Almost immediately the NP was faced with the first of many financial crises. It wasn't until February 1870 that construction was begun with the driving of the first spike at Thompson's Junction near Duluth, Minnesota.

It was heck of a time to build a railroad though. Construction proceeded slowly in the 1870s, slowed and sometimes stalled by such obstacles as the financial panic of 1873, political intrigue, financial finagling, Indian threats, geographic barriers, corporate infighting and power struggles.

But by the summer of 1883, the rails from east and west were ready to be connected. Northern Pacific President Henry M. Villard saw to it that the connection was to be made in style. He organized the "Gold Spike" Excursion – four trains from the east, one from the west. They were to meet in the vast wilds of Montana Territory. With the NP footing the bill, more than 400 guests from the east rode in some of the most elegant roiling stock on wheels.

The guest list read like a "Who's Who" in fields of commerce, finance, government, science and literature. Among guests were former President Ulysses S. Grant, Secretary of the Interior H.M. Teller, journalist Joseph Pulitzer, governors from states and territories served by the NP, and many more. There were even two 30-plus delegates from Germany and England.

Ironically, the actual linking of east and west took place August 22, 1883. Because of the plans for the Villard excursion, word of the August event wasn't given to the eastern media.

Although tracks were in place, Gold Creek wasn't the easiest place to reach. In fact, it was downright dangerous. Tunnels through Bozeman and Mullan passes were not yet completed, so steep, twisting, temporary switchbacks were constructed up and over the two mountainous passes.

Two mishaps delayed the original spike driving ceremony by a day. A rail turned as the lead section of the Iron Horse caravan rounded a sharp curve on the Bozeman Pass switchback and set part of Villard's train on the ground. No one was hurt but the trains were delayed several hours.

Next, it was General Grant's section's turn. On the Mullan Pass switchback a coupling snapped. Some cars in the back part of the train separated from the front half and rolled backward down the four degree grade into the engine of the following section. The British minister and seven of his staff were shaken, none seriously. But the car was seriously damaged, resulting in more delay.

In the meantime, people converged on the Gold Creek site from all directions by varied means – ankle express, travois, coaches, buggies and horseback. The crowd was estimated from 3,000 to 5,000. At the site, a pine bough-bedecked pavilion with seating for more than a thousand persons had been constructed. A plank platform reached to the roadbed where the final thousand feet of track would be laid.

Finally the trains began arriving – the special from the west was first. The Army's Fifth Regiment Band serenaded the crowds; six cannons were in place, ready to boom salutes at the appropriate time.

By mid-afternoon, the ceremonies began. Preceding the laying of track were speeches by NP officials, visiting dignitaries, government spokesmen and General Grant. Then came the race between east and west track laying crews to see who would be first to reach the last spike site. The east crew's rail car was pulled by a huge, black horse, just as he had done since leaving Mandan, Dakota Territory. The west's car derailed enabling the east to win.

At last it was time for the driving of the last spike. There are varying accounts of who participated in the actual spike driving. Consensus is that the first and last licks were administered by H.C. Davis, the man who had also driven the first spike at Thompson's Junction in 1870. Interestingly, the spike was the same one he had driven in Minnesota 13 years earlier.

Davis's official status is clouded by different reports. Among other things, he was identified as "a general utility man for the NP traffic department," "assistant general passenger agent for the NP," and still other witnesses said he was employed in 1883 by the St. Paul, Minneapolis and Manitoba Railroad. The September 1883 edition of *The Northwest* lists Davis with the latter company in the official register of the Villard entourage.

The last spike event was wired for instant news coverage, 1883-style. The spike and the maul were connected by a copper wire to a single strand of telegraph wire. As contact was made, a signal was sent racing eastward and westward to inform the distant public of the great happening.

But nature intervened. Just as the spike was struck, lightning hit a telegraph pole near Billings and broke the connection. The signal did reach St. Paul where it triggered a cannon shot which set off a chain reaction of pealing church bells and blowing steam whistles.

New York and Boston never received the signal.

But the mission had been accomplished. The Northern Pacific Railroad had opened the doorway to a vast new frontier with a ribbon of steel that tied east and west.

100th anniversary of the driving of the last spike at Gold Creek was celebrated with a reenactment in 1983.
Paul Fugleberg photo

The Bearmouth train robberies

Lightning may or may not strike twice in the same place – but train robbers struck three times in roughly the same place about two miles east of Bearmouth, Montana, on the Northern Pacific's mainline. The first train heist was in 1902, the second in 1904 and the third and final time in 1905.

The most detailed description of the three holdups was in 1904. Right on time, near 11 p.m., June 16, 1904, the eastbound Northern Pacific North Coast Limited pulled up to the water tower at the mining community of Bearmouth, about midway between Missoula and Helena, Montana. The fireman, L.S. Reed, descended from the cab as Engineer Thomas H. Wade remained at his post. Two trainmen carrying lanterns were at the far ends of the train but failed to see two armed, masked men lurking in the darkness. Yet all was routine – until the train was ready to pull out.

What happened next is contained in the deposition of one of the robbers – George M. Hammond, alias George H. Wilson and Frank Hammond Miller – after his arrest several weeks later in Spokane, Washington.

Hammond said, "Just as the train was going to pull out we went up and covered the engineer and then we got into the engine. I said to him …'I'm, a man, every inch, and we are going to treat you square – don't run off or anything and you will be all right. Whatever you do, don't run off. Then I asked the fireman if he had a gun and he said no, and I says, 'you do just as we say and you won't get hurt, and when I say stop, you stop the train.'"

Engineer Wade complied and the train pulled away from the water tank. About one-and-a half- miles to the east, Hammond ordered the engineer to stop the train. Then he ordered the two crew members to accompany him and his partner, John Christie, back to the express car.

"The engineer was uneasy about the engine," Hammond said, afraid that the boiler would burn up. Christie suggested that the fireman stay and tend to the engine. Then engineer agreed.

The robbers, armed with knives, a revolver and a Winchester rifle, accompanied the engineer to the express car. Hammond said, "We had the engineer tell the fellows to come out. He knocked on the door said, "Come out, boys, come out for God's sake for my protection, but don't shoot. I am here. Don't shoot." But they wouldn't come out. There wasn't a sound.

"So, I says to my partner, 'Here, put that under the door' and I handed him a bomb. We had given the engineer a cigar in the meantime and told him to light the fuse from his cigar, but it wouldn't light, and then we had some matches with us and got [it] lit by a match and it blowed the door open."

The express agent still didn't come out, but the train electrician appeared at the end of the car. Hammond said, "Get back … don't come out that way, come out the side door. I was afraid he had a gun… He didn't say a word. I thought all the time it was the messenger and he had a gun, so I pulled up my gun – I didn't want to shoot him, though. I would give him a chance. I didn't shoot around the car, but I just fired kind of glancing up the end of the car to scare him. Fired three times to warn him to get back … but he never said a word."

Finally, the electrician came out but the express messenger was still inside. Hammond and the engineer both told him to come out. The messenger answered several times. Hammond said, "He came to the door three or four times … and he had his shotgun right in his hands, stood in the doorway and he says, 'how many are out there?' The engineer says, 'God almighty knows how many there are out here! You better come out. I am in a great a position here. Don't shoot.'"

Still the messenger wouldn't come out so Hammond told the engineer, "Here's another bomb, blow him up. That kind of took the starch out of the messenger and he put up his hands and came out. We searched him and then told them to get up."

The robbers and the train men climbed into the express car. Hammond ordered the messenger to open the safe, adding, "Don't tell me you can't for I've seen you do it. We want you to open that door and no monkey business goes – that's all there's to it. I had seen him open it several times in Missoula. So he opened the out-side door and then he said he had no way to open the inside one. It was combination."

Hammond took his word for it. He said, "So we put the powder right up against it … Thirty-six big sticks, so then I wouldn't ask the messenger to do anything – he had too much nerve. The engineer was the most scared. We told the engineer to lay that bomb there – there was a sixteen-inch fuse. We told him to light the fuse and we would have plenty of time to get out of the car. Told him just as soon as he lit it to get out. So he lit the fuse and we jumped out, the messenger, he started to run and I says, 'Hold on there, you got plenty of time.'

"Just as we got to the engine the blast went off. I told the engineer and the messenger to get right close up to the engine. Didn't want them to get hurt and there might be some splinters flying around."

After the ear-shattering blast the men returned to the express car. Hammond said, "We looked all round and the safe was gone, but I seen the hole in the bottom of the car and I says to my partner, "Look there, that safe is in the ditch.' So he ran out to the bank to look for it, and just then the grass blazed up – caught fire and made it bright there and he ran out to look and I called him back and gave him a cussing and says, 'Make them do your work, don't run out like that in the light.'"

The engineer and the messenger went through the motions of looking but they couldn't see it. Hammond told them, "You fellows can't see nothing. I can see ten miles where you can see two feet. Just then I seen the safe setting there in the ditch."

At first the safe appeared unopened and they thought they'd have to blast it again, But it was open -- wide open.

Hammond said, "I seen the gold coin was all scattered loose on the bottom of the safe and the greenbacks and papers was all tied in packages. It was crammed full of papers and stuff." The robbers picked up all the loose coins.

"We wasn't there a very long time," Hammond said; "The messenger was sitting right down on the ground and the engineer and fireman was taking care of the engine. Then we struck out; we went right down alongside the train and we told the engineer to holler to the conductor not to shoot. He was so exhausted and out of wind he couldn't hardly holler."

So Hammond yelled for him, "Don't shoot, here's the crew. If you shoot you'll kill your own man."

The only shots that were fired happened when the robbers reached the end of the train and Hammond shot out one of the train's marker lamps. Hammond said, "I went around to get a shot at the other one, but that heavy glass, you know, my gun wouldn't phase it. A forty-one wasn't heavy enough. My partner took a shot at it; just then someone stepped out the back of the car. The messenger said, 'Don't shoot. This is the crew. You will only kill us' and this fellow that stepped out says, 'Oh, we won't shoot.'

"I turned to my partner and says, 'There's a cool-headed man. I can tell by the tone of his voice.' Then we went right down the track until we got down two or three hundred yards and we told them to start back, told them not to look around, so then they went back and we lit out."

Thus started the pair's cross-country adventure as they tried to elude bloodhounds, posses, sentries posted on mountain passes and bridges. At first, the robbers showed signs of real ingenuity but their caper soon degenerated into more of a Laurel and Hardy episode.

Hammond explained how they kept hounds from following them and how they made their initial getaway: "We had some liquid we put on our shoes and clothing. When the hounds strike the trail, all they can smell is that liquid and they couldn't follow it. Well, we went right across then to the river. Before that train had pulled out, we had taken a boat and went down about three-quarters of a mile and then we tied the boat there at the embankment. We [had] got a boat, just before the train come to this section house. We were careful not to make any tracks into the river. Just walked on the grass until we come to a plank we had there, and then walked on the plank and jumped into the boat.

"Then we followed the river about ten or fifteen miles, I guess, and then it was daybreak. We quit the boat, then we went a few miles, maybe four or five down the river, and then went up the hill … got into a place where trees were pretty thick … and commenced to see how much coin was in the packages. We left the papers right there, took what stuff we had and struck up the hill and camped."

Drawing on their five-day supply of rations, they breakfasted on coffee and crackers and then struck out again and kept going until about 11 p.m. "We was pretty nearly exhausted," he told authorities. "It was a terribly hot day. We came to a little ravine, had bushes along there and I thought there was water" But there wasn't. The pair hiked along the ravine to a bridge. "I knew there was water on top, so we got up there and found a good spring. The prettiest little spring I ever saw in my life"

Hammond and Christie had supper there, slept for a while, and then were on their way again by 3 a.m., after drinking all the water they could and eating breakfast "We struck out and come out right over that mountain and followed that range."

They headed generally westward across the mountains to the top of another range and followed it along down to the point where it crosses Rock Creek.

"We laid down and slept there then, and along about 10 o'clock I heard something, and I knew it was a mountain lion. Heard it right close – only about 15 feet away from us, but I couldn't see him. He was right above, right on the side of the mountain. We could look up there and see his eyes, see them sparkle. It was terrible dark. I took a shot at him. I know these mountain lions and it kind of took the starch out of me for a minute. My partner, he was scared to death."

Hammond watched the cat's eyes and then shot again but missed. "He never moved," he said. "Just sat right still, then I turned loose at him with the six-shooter, but I couldn't hit him… could just see his eyes, and wasn't sure it was his eyes. I was pretty tired and I laid down then. He didn't bother me any, but my partner couldn't sleep a wink. I slept along until about three o'clock in the morning, and just as it was light enough to see, he [the cat] went off."

The men hiked from about 4 to 9 a.m. until they reached Rock Creek. Hammond said, "I knew this place would be guarded and my partner was pretty tired. We were both pretty well played out."

They agreed that one would sleep and one would stand guard. Christie slept first, about four hours, woke up and told Hammond he'd slept enough and would keep watch. Hammond emphasized, "Whatever you do, don't lay down and go to sleep. Keep your eyes open, and don't go looking around up here at all or they may see you with glasses."

There was no brush or cover at the top of the mountains and movement could be detected from a long way off. Hammond said, "I laid down and went to sleep, but I felt like I couldn't just trust him. I was afraid he wouldn't keep guard." As he awoke he decided to "see if that fellow is asleep. I looked over and see him laying there. I never said a word. There he was, just sound asleep. I never said a word but just went over and got the Winchester. It was right over there about ten feet from his back … and come right down in front of him quietly and I said, 'Here is both of us in your hands and you fast asleep – you sleeping like a hog and don't seem to give a dang whether we're killed or captured or not. Now if you can't keep awake, let me know and I'll stay awake and let you sleep. Don't you ever go to sleep while I am asleep again.' I never caught him asleep after that."

After following a ravine down to Rock Creek they were dismayed to find the stream so wide. Hammond told Christie, "It's impossible to cross here at night. Maybe we can cross in the daytime, but we can't cross any bridge for every bridge will be guarded sure. Then we noticed a house back there from the creek – a big house and it looked like all the windows was all nailed up, like it was deserted."

Hammond and Christie cautiously checked out the scene only to find a man standing by a corner of the house. Hammond told Christie, "They are guarding this place. Let's get away from here as quick as we can; so we went around back and came to the river and thought we could swim it. We strapped our knapsacks on and we started in. When we got about thirty feet I saw we couldn't make it, and had to come back.

"Well, we went up the side of the hill and went to drying our clothes. My partner, he looked over at this house and saw a man just going into this house."

They took the opportunity to get moving again, back up the mountain side. "Must have gone up about 16,000 feet," Hammond exaggerated. "Come to snow, and then we come down on the other side of the mountain. We found a cabin there and watched until the fellows went off, and then we went down and cooked a good meal. We hadn't had anything for three days. He [Christie] stood guard and I went in and cooked, and then I watched while he ate. We left half-a-dollar there. We didn't want to leave a big lot of money for fear they would suspect something. We washed up everything nicely, put everything back in place, and cleaned up everything and shut the door."

As they left they heard sheep bleating ahead and they figured the cabin occupants were sheepherders. Hammond and Christie hid in the bushes. Hammond said, "We was six or seven days out then, and had traveled about sixty miles from the river. We laid down in the bushes there and had some sleep. I kept by eyes open and I could hear men talking all day long. I didn't know whether they were sheepherders or what they were doing. Didn't see anything, but I could hear more talking. Just about dusk, I caught a glimpse of two men – I noticed they had white shirts and they were walking along at a pretty good rate, keeping very quiet."

Hammond surmised they were guards. Then he noticed five more men coming back to the camp. He said, "I never seen five men with a band of sheep before. I was sure they was guards."

The train robbers changed course again. This time they headed across the range and came down into a valley along the edge of a creek and found signs of more searchers. Hammond commented, "Along the edge of the creek, I seen the track of a horse's foot – looked like it was shod."

Back up the mountain again. They hiked close to the top of the range before coming down to the river and following it for several miles. Hammond said, "We intended to build a raft to cross then river, so we got some logs together and strapped our things on our back. We went down the river maybe about fifty yards and the raft struck a big rock and went right up in the air, threw us both off in the water. I had the Winchester and had a knapsack and had the gold coin. Altogether I had about ninety pounds on me and then getting wet, you know, and that water was just like ice. But he [Christie] grabbed me right here by the neck and jerked me back onto the raft and we stuck there on the snag about thirty feet from shore."

Disgusted, Hammond told Christie, "This is poor management all the way through. You are to blame for this, but he just went to cussing and then he commenced to throw our stuff back to the shore. He took the Winchester and threw it across. We saw we would have to get back to the same shore again, so we threw everything back that we could and then we struck out. I had to pole myself along. I was afraid to swim for hitting my knees on the rock, and this leg ain't as strong as the other one anyway. I was crippled in it, haven't got the strength."

Christie, despite being a strong swimmer, drifted downstream before catching hold of some bushes and was helped out by Hammond.

"We sat down, made up our minds we would have to get across on a bridge," Hammond explained. "We'll cross the bridge or get killed, either one." They crossed the Bitterroot River without incident and took off cross-country again. Tempers began to surface. Hammond said that Christie complained that "I was out-traveling him. I says, 'Come along; we will go fast now until we get up into the range, and then we can go it slower.'

"We were pretty well on the range and stopped to rest. He had about one thousand in greenbacks. Now I says, 'Here's a hundred in gold and I talked about what my share was.'"

That led to a mutual cussing match and finally Hammond searched for his gun and told his partner to shut up. "I been square with you. Now if you don't want to give it to me, you won't ever want to. I wanted him to turn over a hundred dollars right there. Then he says, 'I am going to leave you right here. I won't stay with you.'"

Hammond told him, "There's no use talking that way – that's a poor way to do. That's the way children do. I am a man and I want to be used as a man and I want you to do what's right. I'm not trying to kill you. I could have killed you 50 times if I wanted to. I don't want to kill a man for money, nothing of that kind. I would have killed you there when you was asleep – when you were sound asleep and I had to poke you in the belly with the Winchester to wake you up and scare you so you wouldn't look out. I am a man and I want you to stop abusing me. No sir, he wouldn't do it. He said he [wouldn't] stay with me another minute."

Hammond swore at Christie and told him to go on and not to ever let him see him again. "I could have killed him just like a fly, but I never killed any man and I don't want that laid to me, so I let him go. I went down by the mouth of the canyon and had my six-shooters and I found some of his tracks by the river. I knew he was making for Spokane.

Hammond hiked back to Missoula and boarded the westbound train for Spokane. Within a day he crossed paths with Christie again. "I knew him right off. He was shaved up and disguised pretty good. Had his hair cut so you couldn't hardly know him, but I knew him as soon as I saw his eyes. I told him the best thing he could do would be to get out of here and he had not better flash too much money around."

The Hammond-Christie encounter in Spokane eventually led to their arrest. Both men, it turned out, were staying in the same rooming house. Also staying there was Richard Pritchard, a Northern Pacific brakeman. Christie came to Hammond's room about 11 a.m. and stayed for a couple hours and then Hammond went downtown to eat.

Hammond told Christie that the brakeman suspected him [Christie] and that he'd better go. He stayed until 3 or 4 p.m. and then left, telling Hammond he was "going to Frisco."

Next morning about 9, Hammond was still asleep when the brakeman pounded on his door. Hammond said, "The brakeman come in and got to using bad language, talking pretty loud." After getting dressed, Hammond said, "I started downstairs. I asked him to come along, didn't care for his company anyway."

Waiting at the foot of the stairs were Spokane detectives Martin J. Burns and R.T. Briley along with Sheriff W.J. Boust. They all went to Hammond's room where they found 17 of the diamonds that had been taken in the train robbery.

After that Hammond was quite cooperative. He described Christie, 5'10" or 5'11", black curly hair, no mustache, a scar between the base of the thumb and index finger on the left hand. He admitted that both he and Christie were involved in the train robbery and that no others were involved. Hammond said the ammunition, dynamite and the Winchester were purchased in the Helena area, that the gun he used he'd had for seven or eight years, and that the masks used were made from black shirts. He said the rest of the shirts were burned along with papers at the robbery scene.

The sheriff asked, "Mr. Hammond, you stated at the time of the explosion that a valise containing some cotton clothing caught fire and in order to prevent the car taking fire from the burning cloth, you instructed the express messengers and engineer to climb inside the car and extinguish the blaze, did you?"

"Yes."

"What was your object in doing this?"

"I did not want to destroy the railroad property and endanger the lives of any passengers."

Hammond agreed to plead guilty and face sentencing on the robbery charges and to waive extradition to Montana. The NP train carrying Hammond back to Montana also pulled the private car of NP general manager, Harry Horn. When Horn learned that the train robber was aboard, he invited him to have lunch with him in the private car.

Author Eugene Block in *Great Train Robberies of the West* wrote, "It was a strange spectacle – the railroad manager and the train bandit seated together in casual talk. Hammond appeared dejected and squirmed uneasily in his chair. Horn, taking a fatherly attitude, said he hoped that Hammond ultimately would change from an enemy to a friend of the Northern Pacific. Hammond promised that he would."

Hammond was sentenced to 15 years for the robbery and to one year for grand larceny. The latter sentence expired May 26, 1914, but Hammond was paroled on April 8, 1908, and no record is given of where he went afterwards.

Christie, instead of going to San Francisco, went to his home near Hope, North Dakota, where he met his wife and went with her to St. Paul; Minnesota. On his return from St. Paul to Castle, North Dakota, he said, "I met Sheriff Pepper of Steed County, with whom I am well acquainted, and he picked me up."

Christie served his time in the state pen from Sept. 22, 1904, to his parole on July 2, 1908. There is no record of him running afoul of the law either.

1902 robbery was the most tragic

The 1902 incident was the most tragic as the robber killed the engineer and remained uncaught. On Thursday, October 3, 1902, the North Coast Limited was stopped by an unknown robber, apparently working alone. Engineer Dan O'Neal tried to wrest the gun away from the holdup man, but as they grappled in the engine's cab in the darkness, O'Neal was shot and fatally wounded. The robber then went on with his efforts to break into the express car and steal whatever valuables he thought were in it.

Although he pretty well wrecked the car, the outlaw failed to obtain any booty and fled from the scene. Despite efforts of lawmen and bloodhounds in a widespread search, no trace of the robber was ever found.

The New York Times on October 25, 1902, told a different version of the robbery. *The Times* reported that witnesses said eight men took part and that the express and mail cars were rifled and an undetermined amount of cash and valuables were taken. The newspaper also reported that the robber boasted that he had taken part in the robbery of a Southern Pacific train in Oregon the previous year.

In giving details about Engineer O'Neal, *The Times* stated he had a "comfortable house in Missoula, a loving wife, and five children; no one expected him to risk his life to prevent one of his trains from being taken over by a gang of outlaws."

The only clue found, according to *The Times* was a "mask worn by one of the robbers; it was found on a mountain trail about two miles from the scene."

On October 24, 1902, the NP offered a $2,500 reward for the capture of the robber – or a total of $5,000 if two were involved. If more than two robbers took part, the reward would be $2,000 for each of them, with a total of $5,000 for all.

A telegram to Harry Horn, NP general manager in St. Paul, Minnesota, stated that the railroad company would "guarantee expenses of sheriff's posse up to $1,000 to be deducted from reward should they succeed; otherwise company stands expenses."

Neither the extensive search nor the reward money resulted in catching the crook or crooks.

Robber had a bad time in 1905 caper

Not quite a year after the 1904 heist the North Coast Limited Train No. 2 was again victimized in the Bearmouth area. Various newspaper accounts initially had reports of up to eight robbers involved, a large sum of cash stolen, the robber critically injured, and the engineer and the express messenger cast in the roles of heroes.

When fact and fiction finally were sifted out, it turned out to be one robber -- Clarence B. Young, 24, working alone. He was not injured as badly as first thought. No money was stolen although the express car and safe were damaged. Both the engineer, George L. Wilson (coincidentally, the same first and last times of one of the 1904 train robbers) and the messenger, George L. Laub, received $1,000 rewards from the Northern Pacific, but the messenger's official account complained about the role played by the engineer.

Despite the flowery and speculative newspaper accounts, brief telegraph dispatches between Northern Pacific officials seemed to carry the most concise account of what happened. The initial wire was issued at 3:35 a.m., May 28, 1905, to various stations along the main line. It read, "No. 2 held up two and one-half miles east of Bearmouth at 11:20 p.m., explosions were heard. No particulars yet. Am starting posses from Deer Lodge, Missoula and Drummond. Will report further when obtain more particulars." Andrew Gibson, NP superintendent, Missoula.

Two hours later, Gibson wired the rest of the story: "No. 2 was held up about 11:20 p.m., two miles east of Bearmouth at mile post 81 by one man we know of and think there was one more but not sure about there being two.

"He had about 25 pounds of dynamite and blew safe open in express car, shattering sides. Blew door off and when the third explosion went off, he made Engineer Wilson get in car ahead of him and the messenger to follow him; just as he and the engineer got in the car he had the engineer light a match and Engineer Wilson saw a chance for the messenger to hit him and blew out the match, and the messenger struck him with a piece of the broken car in back of head and layed (sic) him out.

"We have robber tied, he is alive and will take him to Drummond where we will turn him over to the county authorities. Express car is in shape to go through to Butte where transfer can be made. Will have diligent search made for the second man. Trainmen think there was a second man and should be able to get him before long if there was one. No valuables of anything reported taken and passengers not disturbed. Only damage is to side of car."

On May 29, Gibson wired, "Train robber has regained consciousness, but will not talk about himself. Will not tell his name and positively denies having a partner in the crime. Special agents Goodard and Hindman are on the way to Phillipsburg (sic) to see if they extract any information from him."

Gibson's final wire was sent June 7 stating, "Clarence B. Young arraigned in District Court Phillipsburg yesterday p.m. Pleaded guilty to holding up Train No. 2 two miles east of Bearmouth … Waived statuary (sic) time for hearing sentence passed and was sentenced to 50 years in the State Penitentiary at Deer Lodge, Mont., where he will be taken today."

An interesting aspect of the incident is the big difference in the messenger's statement to the press shortly after the capture of the bandit and the report he filed with the express company while aboard Train No. 3 on May 29.

The press reported quoted him as crediting Engineer Wilson with a major role in the capture: … "Before the man hit the floor, Engineer Wilson seized the gun, which was strapped to the robber's wrist and the victory was ours … George Wilson kept his head from first to last and at all times was cool and collected. Of course, we had no opportunity to speak to each other or even to look into each other's eyes, but somehow I had a premonition that if the opportunity came Wilson would be there with the goods, and sure enough he was. From first to last the engineer showed not the slightest sign of fear or excitement … When he had secured the guns, Wilson went to the side of the car and yelled to Conductor Sires telling him to come forward …"

But in his report to Northern Pacific Express Co. Superintendent W.S. Hay in St. Paul and to M.G. Hall in Portland, Laub stated: "…As the robber bent over slightly to look into the safe I saw the chance I was looking for, and as I drew back my left arm, it came in contact with a piece of the wreckage which I grabbed and hit the robber on the side of the head, then hit him with my right hand and grabbed him at the same time. This second blow knocked his head against the safe. I followed up on my advantage by embracing him, getting ahold of his two wrists and held him tight.

"I naturally expected the Engineer would stand by me, but when the first blow was struck he disappeared which left me with the robber having guns in both hands and still fighting. I called and insisted for the Engineer to come back to take the guns out of the robber's hands, which he finally did after which he got out of the car, taking the guns with him. I called for him to come back again, also for the train crew. After what seemed a considerable space of time, the Engineer returned, but in the meantime I had put the robber out of business.

"I had the Engineer hold the robber's hands while I got my shotgun, in case there should be any assistance to the robber from outside, feeling confident that I could take care of one or two more of them ..."

On June 1, J.M. Hannaford, Vice President of the Northern Pacific Express Company, mailed a copy of Laub's official report to General Manager Horn with this terse cover letter: "Thinking you might be interested in same, I enclose you herewith personal report made by messenger Geo. H. Laub in the matter of the last Bearmouth holdup."

Despite the conflicting reports, both men received $1,000 rewards and letters of congratulations and appreciation from the Northern Pacific Railway. Both men wired their thanks. Laub said, "Thank you for your generous appreciation of my attempt to do my duty. Did the best I could under the circumstances." Three days later, he sent a telegram to NP Vice President Hannaford: "I wish to express my sincere thanks to the Management of the Railway Company and the Northern Pacific Express Company for the liberal gift, I also wish to say that I greatly appreciate your letter of commendation and the good words received from the other officers."

Wilson's acknowledgment was brief: "Your wire received, I appreciate very much the expressions contained therein and thank you for your generosity."

With the third Bearmouth train robbery resolved quickly and without a fatality, the editor of the *Anaconda Standard* and the Northern Pacific management engaged in a tongue-in-cheek exchange of the possibility of scheduling holdups on an annual basis as a tool to provide good news stories.

In a letter dated June 8, 1905, NP General Manager Horn wrote to J.H. Durston, Editorial Manager for the *Standard:* "The other day I wrote you what was intended to be a sincere appreciation of your paper on the Union Depot proposition at Butte, but since writing that letter I have been more impressed with your issue of May twenty-ninth and June fourth.

"You did very well with the depot, no complaints to make, nothing but praise, but I think you have made the country famous with your issues on the Bearmouth holdup. I do not know whether you need one of these every year in order to get in special matter or not. I think we can put them in once a year, provided that the cost does not run any higher than the last one and we can get anything like the sendoff that was given by your edition of May twenty-ninth and June fourth. It is a little early to talk about making contact with your paper to furnish Bearmouth holdup news once a year.

"In case you can throw some light on this proposition, or have some alternative scheme to suggest, I would be glad to hear from you, but anyway, I want to congratulate you on the way you do things and put them up to the public."

Obviously no arrangement was forthcoming – nor were there any other Bearmouth train robberies.

A fiery arrival

Simply trying to reach Polson could be a harrowing experience in 1910. Golden E. Bibee was among early settlers who arrived at the north end of Flathead Lake via the Great Northern and then to Polson by boat. As the train skirted the southern edge of new Glacier National Park, forest fires raged on all sides. Golden wrote: *It looked like the world was on fire. A pilot engine ran ahead of our train ... The night was dark but most of the way the forest fire lighted the coaches like day...*

Somewhere in the middle of the burn the train stopped and several people came aboard. One young mother apologized to my wife because her children had whooping cough. She said they had had a very narrow escape and were very thankful to get away from the fire alive.

The boat trip from Somers to Polson was no less hazardous. The Bibees were aboard the *City of Polson* when the boat became lost in the smoke. As if the smoke weren't bad enough, a windstorm struck as they were half-way down the lake:

The waves grew wilder and the wind stronger causing the smoke to sting the eyes intensely. My little family clung together and hung on. My wife was too seasick to care whether the ship went down or not... I wondered how Captain Swanson could keep his eyes open to see at all. The engines slowed down and the crew seemed uneasy. There was much consultation -- we were facing the storm, bouncing like a cork on the waves. For some time we barely held our own. Then the squall stopped as suddenly as it had begun. The sun disappeared behind a mountain and darkness came on sudden and intense...

Then came the search for the shoreline and the Narrows. How this was accomplished I'll never understand. I couldn't see the bow of the boat. The squall seemed to have thickened the smoke rather than clear it.

The boat crept through the Narrows safely, sped up and pretty soon slowed down again, as the captain successfully groped for the dock, guided by the electric plant whistle.

Flathead's Paper Railroads

Preceding completion of the Northern Pacific Railway's successful branch line from Dixon to Flathead Lake, there was considerable jawboning, planning, dreaming and promoting what amounted to no more than the western Montana's "paper railroads."

Instead of dependable passenger and freight service, their trademarks were announcements, speculation, surveys, planning and plotting, fund raising, politicking and more. But the bottom line was that they never got off the newsprint as far as additional rail service to this area was concerned.

Among the paper railroads were proposals by two well established roads, the Milwaukee and the Great Northern, plus Colonel A. A. White's Missoula-Finley Point electric line, a joint GN-NP connecting venture, a Columbia Falls-Whitefish to Polson electric railroad, a Columbia Falls to Bigfork route, a Milwaukee route from Lewistown to Spokane via Great Falls, Bigfork and Kalispell, a Kalispell to Polson electric line, and W. A. Clark's proposal for a Missoula to Polson electric line. As late as 1921 the NP was exploring plans to electrify its trains in this area with power from the Flathead River.

In June 1910 the local media ran articles telling of the Milwaukee and Great Northern both looking toward Polson. The GN was reported working for acquisition of right-of-way from Somers to the east shore and south. Milwaukee's chief engineer and others were making cursory examinations through the Mission Valley and the NP was exploring a route from Dixon north.

The *Lakeshore Sentinel* reported "It is also well known that the Northern Idaho and Montana Power Co. have authorized Mr. Wall to go ahead with improvements in Polson that will mean the expenditure of more than one hundred thousand dollars during the present summer. Adding these facts together, one can only get the following answer: The Milwaukee road intends building a line to this point, and the Northern Idaho & Montana Power company is getting in shape to care for the great increase of population that the coming of a railroad will bring to Polson ..."

Apparently a local company was formed to build a Whitefish-Polson line. A 1910 report in the *Kalispell Bee* said "After ten months of persistent work of getting right-of-way, the directors of the Whitefish-Polson electric railway have now secured enough of the route to feel justified in going ahead with the work, and are this week to make the first offer of stock to the public."

It was reported that 90 percent of the right-of-way between Whitefish and Cramer's Landing on the west shore of Flathead. Lake was secured. Largest portion of it was donated by farmers. Intent was to sell a sufficient block of stock to people living in the valley to build the first section either from Whitefish to Kalispell or from Kalispell to Polson. With that part of the routing complete, funding would be obtained by a bond issue to complete the next section -- and to extend it to Missoula, Camas Hot Springs, and to other valley locations.

By December 1910, it appeared as if Polson would have electric inter-urban service coming at it from both sides of Flathead Lake. The Dec. 20, 1910, *Daily Inter Lake* reported "Dirt will be flying on an electric railway that will run down the east side taking in Bigfork and the east shore of the lake by the time the present Congress has closed its doors, if nothing goes wrong with the apparently well laid plans of James A. Talbott [and] a number of Flathead people from Bigfork and Butte businessmen. . .

"The plans were laid at Columbia Falls last Thursday and Friday when a number of men gathered to talk over the feasibility of tapping the east side and putting a trolley trunk north and south through the county. Practically $100,000 is said to have been tentatively pledged to the pushing of the enterprise.

"Columbia Falls would be the northern terminal of the road and Polson its southern. A power plant to be located on the east side is to furnish power for operating the cars. . ."

The Whitefish & Polson Electric Line would come down the west shore. The *Flathead Courier* on Dec. 23, 1910, reported "This company now has the right-of-way from Whitefish to Somers nearly all secured, has $100,000 in stock already subscribed and the officers are planning on getting operations started at once. They want the people of Polson and vicinity to help by taking stock in the enterprise. . . The subscriptions of stock would be held until the company has proved that it intends to 'come through' with the road."

In September 1911, Charles W. Clark announced that work on the preliminary survey for an extension of the Missoula Electric Line from Missoula to Polson would be started at once.

A Polson Chamber of Commerce delegation in November 1911 went to Missoula to learn about W. A. Clark's Missoula-Polson railroad scheme. Ironically, F. L. Gray, M. A. Myhre and A. W. Pipes arrived too late for the banquet -- their train was behind schedule. But they got there in time for the speeches.

They reported . . . "it seems very sure that Missoula is to be connected with the wonderful Flathead country by bands of steel, for last evening W. A. Clark promised that he would do what he could to help the project, which contemplated a line from Missoula to Polson. . ."

There was an abrupt stop to all but Colonel White's railroad planning in 1915. But the NP brought railroad dreams to reality when its rails reached Polson in December 1918.

Northern Pacific engine 1356 can now be seen at the Missoula depot.

(Paul Fugleberg photo)

No. 1356 -- the engine that kept coming back

If ever a steam locomotive earned a reputation as "the engine that always came back," it's old Northern Pacific No. 1356, on display in a small fenced area near the Missoula, Montana, railroad depot.

Many persons in Montana and Idaho were pulled safely by 1356, sometimes under harrowing conditions. While there is no one left who recall taking the train to safety in 1910 when forest fires raged around them, they probably passed the word down to their children about the traumatic experience. The 1902 Class 5-4 engine and tender pulled its load of passengers through areas of fire on both side of the track and over a wooden trestle that was actually on fire.

The late Ron Nixon of Polson, a retired NP telegrapher, communications manager and photographer, several years ago said that his records showed the engine that had been serving Missoula-Spokane passengers starting in 1902, was replaced about 1907 by Q-Class Pacifics and relegated to freight service.

But 1356 came back during the 1910 forest fires for special assignments. The engine also served rescue missions during the floods of 1932 and snowslides of 1936 – and always came back.

However, on one run of its long freight career, No. 1356 took a long time to return home. On June 20, 1943, as 1356 was pulling 28 cars of logs between Missoula and Hamilton, Montana, over a flood-weakened span over the Bitterroot River near Florence, the bridge collapsed. The engine took a dive and was almost submerged under loads of logs.

Insult was added to injury when NP wrecker 45 derailed and crashed atop 1356 during salvage operations. The wrecker unit had tried to lift the fallen span but overturned when logs were dislodged. The wrecker was dismantled and taken away in pieces.

Finally on June 20, 1943 – its cab smashed beyond recognition – 1356 was lifted from the mud, rerailed and taken to the NP shops in Livingston, Montana. Thirteen months later, the locomotive came back for several more years of service.

Other facts from Nixon's records showed that 1356's most frequent runs were between Missoula and Wallace, Idaho. No. 1356 was a relatively light locomotive but a photo showed it rolled into Missoula from Butte with 100 cars in tow; another photo revealed 1356 atop towering Fish Creek trestle. A 1902 picture showed the engine pulling freight cars across Lake Pend O'Reille near Hope, Idaho; the photo makes you wonder if life preservers were required.

No. 1356 was retired in Missoula on June 5, 1954. But the engine still had one more wild adventure.

When the NP decided to donate a locomotive to the City of Missoula, the late Walter McLeod of Missoula, an NP director, wanted an engine most representative of the community's history. Once again, the call went out for 1356 – just in time, too. The aging locomotive was found in the "deadline" at the South Tacoma scrap heap. The engine was fixed up again, brought back to Missoula and placed in its present setting. An impressive dedication ceremony was held Nov. 10, 1955, despite a heavy, cold rain.

No. 1356 had come back again – this time for the last time.

S-1, the last steamer

This S-1 switch engine was used in the Somers Lumber Company plant in Somers. It was referred to as a "fireless cooker" because its steam supply had to be replenished frequently from a stationary boiler. The S-1 is now at the Miracle of America Museum in Polson and is operated during the Live History Days.

Ron Nixon photo

Personal reflections

Silver cartwheels were great

I wish that those big, old clunky silver dollars were still in circulation in Montana.

The "cartwheels" provided a certain amount of psychological security. When you heard 'em jingling in your pocket, you felt you weren't broke – yet.

They tended to anchor one to Earth when those strong gusty winds blew – especially in areas east of the mountains. They worked good here in the valley on blustery days, too.

Men's store owners liked them because there was always a demand for belts and suspenders among guys who liked to impress people with pockets loaded with silver dollars.

And sewing shop, dry cleaner and laundry operators found they had to replace pockets that were worn out by the weighty coins.

Tourists loved 'em because they were valuable novelties and souvenirs.

But even tradition can be ended by federal decree. Many folks were saddened by the departure of the cartwheels when they were replaced by often wrinkled, dirty and germ-carrying, silent pieces of paper in the form of unglamorous dollar bills.

The remaining silver dollars then became collectors' items. I never had enough to start collecting, but I did carry one around for years during lean economic times to use in case of emergency. And sure enough, I came up 75 cents short after buying the kids ice cream cones and had to use it.

A couple official attempts were made to mint smaller size dollar coins but they never caught on with the public. They simply lacked the weight, feel, sound and character of the cartwheels.

Closest replacement occurred when the late Maynard Nixon taped two half-dollar coins together and used them in his purchases and to make change for customers. That was his personal peaceful protest against the feds' decision to withdraw the silver dollars. His practice lasted only a few days before he was officially warned that might be considered "defacing currency!"

Incidentally, whatever became of the 50-cent pieces? I haven't seen half-dollar coins for a long time.

Numbers are relative things

A lot of folks like the stories that numbers tell … or don't tell.

Politicians kick numbers around to give scenarios that may be pleasing to voters. Their opponents often take the same numbers and make them tell an entirely different story.

Numbers can be a relative thing – f'rinstance, the length of one minute, just 60 seconds, depends on which side of the bathroom door you're standing.

The late John Dutzar used numbers to illustrate man's relative insignificance when compared to the universe. He said that if all of the world's population (estimated at 3 billion in 1960) were packed into a one cubic mile-size box, one could lose it in the vastness of the Grand Canyon of Arizona.

By 1985 the population had increased to around 4.5 billion, and was predicted to hit 6 billion by the year 2000. As a result of coffee break conversation in 1985, Ken Moase did some figuring to prove or disprove Dutzar's theory.

Moase figured that there are 147,197,952,000 cubic feet in a cubic mile. If the average body occupies 8 cubic feet of space, an estimated 4.5 billion population would occupy about 36 billion cubic feet.

One quarter cubic mile, Moase said, equals 36,799,480,000 cubic feet, well within the scope of Dutzar's theory.

Heck, even at today's figures, it looks like the theory is still good.

Author James Michener in his novel *Space* writes that as we sleep, our galaxy moves in relation to all other galaxies in six different directions at an accumulated speed of probably 2.5 million miles an hour. No wonder we're tired when we wake up in the morning.

Sometimes a 50 mph wind gust can nearly knock you off your pins. But scientists say that Earth, rotates and rockets though space at 860 mph but has no effect. I don't know about that. Some days it's a struggle to keep from falling off.

Here's another number we can all easily understand. In school we learned that 100 cents equals $1. Now government economists tell us the dollar is worth only 37 cents – or less.

And I recall a cautionary note in this column in 1998 when I wrote, "Can't help but take this talk about a balanced budget or an actual surplus … with a grain of salt, The balance will soon be out of whack if we get into a shooting war with Iraq."

Finally, in the summer when you get tired of prolonged hot spells, just read the temperatures on the Celsius scale. At least it won't sound as warm.

Oceans of Emotions

You've got 'em, I've got 'em, we've all got 'em. Emotions and feelings.

Perhaps the highest compliment one person can give to another is the ability to share feelings with one another.

For instance, what would a writer do if he couldn't share the feelings of people he was writing about? Or a columnist who can't share his feelings with readers?

If a writer couldn't "feel" the touch of God in a setting of alpine splendor, the rustle of leaves in the wind, the scent of pine on the cool fall air, the sound of a gurgling brook, or the "I've got 'im" yell of an excited youngster as he hooks a scrappy fish. ... If he couldn't "feel" these things, how would he ever communicate effectively?

This applies to almost any occupation and profession, too. A teacher must be able to share students' enthusiasm over accomplishments – and to sense their fears and frustration over failures.

A doctor has to sense his patients' anguish and worry over sickness and the impact on patients' families. And the doctor certainly has to share with them their thankfulness for healing and recovery.

A nurse or nurse's aide must be a very special, caring type of person to communicate well with patients -- some temporarily disabled, some wheelchair-bound, or permanently bedridden, others terminally ill.

And how about a pastor? He or she must be a super-sensitive individual able to share with congregational members their triumphs and tragedies. A policeman, judge, or lawyer all have to really care for people they deal with, some of them quite unlovable at the time of encounter.

Add to the list countless other occupations – firemen, farmers, ranchers, undertakers, psychologists, psychiatrists, politicians, military personnel, employers, employees.

Virtually everyone has feelings and emotions that need to be shared. So the next time you find yourself crying over someone's misfortune, or weeping tears of joy for their good fortune, or your own appreciation of good news ... if you feel a tingle in the spine or a lump in your throat when the band strikes up the school fight song, the national anthem or when you watch the flag pass by – thank God for the ability you have to feel those emotions. Don't be embarrassed or apologize. They're signs that you really care. Care to share those emotions – yours and theirs.

Economics 101

OK, Congressional representatives and senators, listen up:

When the outgo exceeds the income,

the upkeep will be your downfall.

Now I know you believe you understand what you think I said, but I'm not sure you realize that what you heard is not what I meant!

In other words, balance the budget and then budget the balance.

Terah T. Maroney's float plane at the Narrows of Flathead Lake in 1913.

More historic happenings

A cabinet maker, a logger and a farm boy influenced aviation

A cabinet maker, a logger and a farm boy seems like an unlikely trio destined to mold America's aviation future, but they did – beyond even their own dreams

It started when Terah T. Maroney, born in Murfreesboro, Tennessee, in 1880, came to Butte, Montana, in 1908 as a cabinet maker with hopes of becoming a railroad engineer on the Milwaukee or Northern Pacific railroads. But he flunked the railroad exam in Big Timber, Montana. With that dream dashed, he moved to Great Falls, Montana, to work for a sash and door company.

Railroad's loss was aviation's gain, however. It was in Great Falls that he became interested in flying. Maroney built his own airplane and test flew it with some degree of success – a distance of about 300 feet at Great Falls on July 6, 1911. Encouraged, he took parts of that plane and built a second craft, which he flew from a field near the Black Eagle smelter to the bluffs near the present Great Falls airport and returned.

So much for carpentry and railroading. Terah Maroney was hooked on flying. He went to San Diego, California, obtained his pilot's license in March 1912, bought a used Model E Curtiss for $4,500, and returned to Montana where he chalked up a number of state records including a 43-minute sustained flight. State legislators proclaimed him "Montana's Official Aviator."

Maroney soon became Montana's top barnstormer. Among his appearances was an exhibition on Flathead Lake, July 23, 1913, publicized as the "first flight ever made from water in the Pacific Northwest."

The Flathead Courier reported that the Polson area was selected as the flight site "owing to the favorable atmospheric conditions that prevail here, there being no body of water in the country where there is less wind to contend with than there is here."

Maroney selected Idylwilde Island (now known as Big Bull Island) as the base for his flight. He said he would take a lady passenger on one of his two planned flights, and that he would "drop a (flour) bomb on the deck of the (steamer) Klondike to prove the hydroplane's worth in war.

On flight day the weather was lousy – cold, windy and rainy. Many spectators opted not to sail to the site. Despite delays, Maroney lived up to his reputation of never canceling a show. In fact, he made three flights instead of two.

Flathead Courier editor Claude Cowman described the event: "The first flight was made about 3 o'clock when he sailed out over the waters of the main lake and after rising several hundred feet, commenced circling over the islands and the boats.

"The wind kept blowing harder all the time and by the time he struck the water, the waves were running pretty high, but Mr. Maroney did not seem to mind it in the least, and came gliding in across the whitecaps midst a shower of spray…"

The steamer Klondike left before Maroney's second trip, but he caught it ten to twelve miles up the lake and was loudly cheered by the passengers as he circled several times. Maroney's third trip was made towards evening when he took Miss Sadie Cresswell for a short ride.

Despite the weather, the flights were so successful that Maroney planned a second exhibition two weeks later. That show had its embarrassing moments though.

The aviator and his helpers waited all day for the wind to die down so they could leave Idylwilde Island and bring with them their tents, tools and the plane. Early in the evening the wind calmed temporarily and Maroney flew the plane to the west shore site where they had assembled the aircraft before the exhibition. The rest of the crew was to come along in the motorboat.

About an hour later a fire was noted on the lake, near the island. Maroney feared that the gasoline in the boat had caught fire. It would have taken a boat at least a half-hour to reach the fire, so Maroney jumped into his plane and took off toward the fire.

But he was to become rescuee instead of rescuer.

Only four miles out the plane ran out of fuel and Maroney glided to a deadstick landing on the lake. He was rescued by the launch, Eva B, and was towed in the direction of the blaze which turned out to be a signal fire on Little Bull Island. The motor boat's engine had quit and the men pulled ashore.

The plane was left on the island overnight so the Eva B could tow the boat ashore. However, waves swamped the smaller boat and the crew's tent and tools were swept overboard. The tool chest was retrieved with a grappling hook the next day. Two weeks later Maroney returned, saw the tent from the air, and it was retrieved. Although the weather was good this time, the crowds weren't up to expectations, but he made the flights anyway.

Weeks later when Maroney learned that boats owned by the Montana and Clipper companies did not have enough passengers to sail to the exhibition, he refunded the money paid by the firms although he was not legally obliged to do so.

A week after his last Flathead Lake appearance, Maroney crashed during a show in Kellogg, Idaho, and he escaped with bumps and bruises. In true barnstorming tradition, he patched up his plane and himself and kept a promised booking in Butte the next Sunday.

The logger learns to fly

In 1915, Maroney transferred his flight operations to Seattle where he operated a flying school and had a flying boat on Lake Union. Among those he taught to fly was a logger who had become so enthused over the future of aviation that he gave up logging to build airplanes. It was a significant decision. The logger's name was Bill Boeing. His company is still a leader in commercial and military aviation manufacturing.

In 1916 Maroney went to Shreveport, Louisiana, as a civilian flight instructor and army test pilot. After World War I, he moved to Paso Robles, California, and returned to the cabinet making trade and built some houses. But he also kept flying and even flew an airplane for a movie scene in Placerville, California.
He quit the carpentry trade again to work for Cessna Aircraft in East St. Louis, Illinois. On Jan. 12, 1929, Maroney was killed when he got too close to a propeller.

Farm boy's imagination takes flight

The farm boy whose life was touched by Maroney was eight-year-old Leslie Tower, who witnessed Maroney's first flight from Flathead Lake. The idea of flying captured the boy's imagination and never let go.

Setting his sights on a career in aviation, Tower graduated from Polson High School in 1922, took engineering at the University of Washington for a year, then quit to become an army flying cadet. He served at Brooks and Kelly fields in Texas before returning to the University of Washington.

In early 1925 he joined the young Boeing Company as a draftsman and soon began test flying Boeing planes. His career with Boeing was interrupted briefly when he returned to the army for a stint at Langley Field, Virginia. He returned to Boeing in 1927 and until his death in 1935 Tower test flew virtually every new commercial and military aircraft to come off the Boeing drawing boards – pursuits, bombers, mail and passenger planes.

Among the planes was the single engine, five-passenger Boeing Monomail, which flew the Boeing Air Transport's Mountain Division route between Salt Lake City, Utah, and Cheyenne, Wyoming, in 1931. From the Monomail evolved the twin-engine, all metal bomber, the Boeing B-9, the first to have a retractable landing gear. It could fly at 186 miles per hour at 6,000 feet but the pilot still sat in an open cockpit.

The B-9 provided a basic design for a radical new commercial passenger plane, the Boeing 247. When Tower tested that plane he said it had "everything including a kitchen sink" – and the pilot and co-pilot rode inside!

He termed the 247 an "airborne Pullman" that could carry a stewardess, ten passengers, cargo, climb to 11,500 feet on either of its two engines, and cruise at 180 miles an hour. Deeply upholstered seats lined each side of the cabin; by each seat was a large view window. The cabin was heated, ventilated, had dome lights, individual reading lights, a small galley and a complete lavatory.

The cockpit was located ahead of the wing, away from the engines, giving the pilot excellent visibility. Navigational devices included sending and receiving radio telephone equipment, a directional gyro and compass, sensitive altimeter, rate of climb and turn and bank indicators, and an artificial horizon. A full array of gauges helped the pilots, too. One gadget even reminded the pilot to lower the landing gear.

A second edition of the 247 was produced in 1932 – the 247D – and was named the "airplane of the year" and solidified Boeing's reputation as a leading aircraft designer and manufacturer.

As Boeing's chief test pilot Tower was in on the beginning of the next evolution of the 247 – Project 299 – in response to an Army Air Corps call for a multi-engine bomber.

Project 299 took shape rapidly. Within three weeks the basic design was obtained. It called for bombs to be loaded into bomb bays. The pilot and crew were stationed inside – as in the 247. The cockpit was heated, sound-proofed and made reasonably comfortable for long range operation. A record number of defensive machine guns were added. One observer commented that the plane was a virtual "flying fortress."

At 3:42 a.m., Aug. 20, 1935, Boeing's hopes for the future rode with Tower on one of the most important airplane flights ever made as the No. 299 took off from Seattle and headed for Dayton, Ohio. Nine hours and 2,100 miles later, after averaging 233 miles per hour at an average altitude of 12,500 feet, the flight ended in Dayton.

Kind of puny figures today, but that was a record then. Tower told army officials that he had used only 63 percent of the 3,000 available horsepower and that the automatic pilot controls handled the aircraft almost all the way.

Tower remained at Dayton through the testing which convinced officials that the 299 was the bomber of the future. Despite it size – 70 feet long, 105-ft. wing span, and 15 feet high – the plane handled remarkably easy. But because of its size, it was necessary to "lock" the elevator controls when the plane was on the ground to secure it against wind guests. These spring locks were released by the pilot before takeoff.

On Oct. 30, 1935, Tower accepted a last minute invitation by Major Ployer P. Hill, Chief of the Army Air Corps Flight Testing Section, to go along as a passenger. With Major Hill at the controls, the 299 roared down the runway and lifted into the air at an awkward angle. Hill had forgotten to unlock the elevator controls. At 300 feet the plane went into a flat spin, crashed and burned. Major Hill died but the co-pilot, Leslie Tower and two other occupants survived. However, Tower succumbed to his injuries on Nov. 10.

The 299 concept was accepted by the army and evolved into the Boeing B-17 Flying Fortress, a plane that played a significant role in halting the momentum of the Axis powers in World War II.

B-17 Flying Fortress bomber made an unexpected visit to Polson in February 1943. Local residents lined the runway with automobile headlights!

The night WWII came to Polson

Late in the morning of Feb. 5, 1943, a B-17 crew climbed aboard their Flying Fortress bomber near Walla Walla, Washington, for what was supposed to be a two-hour practice bombing run.

It was far from a routine training mission, though. A combination of bad weather, lost radio communications and relative inexperience resulted in a nerve-wracking, nearly 12-hour flight that ended at the Polson, Montana, airport.

At that time the Polson airport had nowhere near the present 4,000 feet of lighted, blacktopped runway. There was barely 2,500 feet of usable runway, no lights, and an unplowed 18 to 24-inch blanket of snow.

After groping aimlessly all afternoon and evening through and over the clouds, the B-17 pilot, Lt. Jim Breeden of Augusta, Montana, finally found fairly decent weather over the Mission and lower Flathead valleys. He brought the plane lower for a closer look and spotted the lights of Ronan, then Polson. He circled Polson several times and tried to pick out a place to land.

Polson telephone operator, Maude Brassfield, had been advised of a missing B-17 earlier. Shortly before 10 a.m., when she heard the circling, low flying bomber, she and operator Louise Malgren, who had seen the plane circling as she came on shift, alerted many residents.

Highway Patrolman Wallace Beaudry and Les P. Baldwin led a caravan of cars to the airport where they lighted the runway with vehicle headlights and handheld flashlights.

It was just in time. Breeden had picked out what appeared to be a fairly flat field south of town for a wheels-up emergency landing. When the crew saw the string of cars lining up along the snow-covered runway, however, their hopes soared.

Breeden made a low level circle around the field, ordered the practice bombs defused and dropped in an open area. Then he brought the big warbird in from the north and made a wheels-down landing with a rooster-tail spray of snow. The deep snow helped brake the aircraft. As the bomber reached the river-end of the runway, the pilot swung the plane around and taxied back to a parking spot opposite the fairgrounds grandstand. Less than five minutes of fuel remained.

A perspiring, much relieved crew piled out. Navigator Lt. Herbert F. Egender's first act was to kiss the ground – snow and all. "Then he removed the secret Norden Bomb Sight from the plane and had it stored in the vault in the Security State Bank.

While deputies guarded the plane, the crew was taken to Polson and treated to an 11 p.m. T-bone steak dinner at Les Baldwin's Hut Café and then bedded down for the night in the Salish Hotel.

For the next couple days the crew was wined, dined and danced royally by hospitable Polsonites. So much so, that the airmen named their plane "The Polson Express" in appreciation. Hundreds of local residents visited the airport to look over their nighttime WWII visitor, which was and still is the largest plane to land and takeoff from the Polson airport. School kids and others were permitted to write their names on the fuselage.

An experienced crew, headed by war hero Major Jim Wheless, was brought to Polson to fly the plane back to Walla Walla. Lake County road equipment was used to clear the runway to its full 2,500 feet and fences were removed. Wheless, however, had the plane airborne in less than 2,100 feet.

In the years since, Colonel Herb Egender returned to visit Polson folks several times. Also the pilot's brother, Vic Breeden of San Marino, California, visited Polson to gather newspaper stories and oral accounts of the incident.

Both men filled in gaps of what happened after The Polson Express and its crew members went to war. Egender said, "We were really lucky that night in 1943. Subsequently, luck ran out for some of the crew. We left Salina, Kansas, on April 17, 1943, and flew to Scotland via Michigan, Maine, Goose Bay, Labrador and Iceland. We then went on to England, left our plane in a depot and joined the 91st Bomb Group as a replacement crew.

"Neapolitano was left home on non-flying status since he suffered terribly from air sickness. As was the custom then, our crew was broken up to give various members experience with seasoned crews. Pilot Jim Breeden was shot down over Kiel on his first mission and was a Prisoner of War. Only a couple of days later, Morris Floyd, our navigator, suffered the same fate over Wilemshaven. The rest of the crew then flew a number of missions with other seasoned pilots.

"On mission No. 7 for our crew," Egender said, "I moved into the lead plane. The rest of the crew was in a plane flying on our left wing over St. Nazaire. They were shot down and only two of the gunners survived.

"That left me as the only one still flying. I dodged the bullet literally until my 15th mission on Aug. 17, 1943. I was shot down on the way to Schweinfurt and taken prisoner. Those of us who were POWs were liberated on April 19, 1945."

Vic Breeden said that his brother was not at the controls of the Polson Express when it was shot down over the Kiel Canal area. The pilot spent the rest of the war on a German POW camp where he had some harrowing experiences: Hunger that he and other prisoners endured along with their guards; a 60-mile march late in the war to flee advancing Russian troops – he said the GIs actually fared better than their guards on the march; and the last POW camp in which Breeden was interned was caught in a firefight between German and American forces.

After the war Breeden was a rancher in the Augusta, Montana, area. Vic Breeden said Jim never cared to talk much about his wartime experiences, but he had a fond place in his heart for Polson folks who came to his rescue by outlining the snow-clogged runway with headlights and flashlights.

Colonel Herb Egender returned several times to Polson in the years following his wartime emergency landing here. Folks he visited included Eddie Pinkney, left, and Les Baldwin, who were among the people who drove their cars and trucks to the Polson airport to light the runway with headlights.

Paul Fugleberg photo

34

Flathead Lake Steamboat Days

There were two parts to the Flathead Lake steamboat era. The first half began shortly after the completion of the Northern Pacific railway in 1883. The second half was marked by the homestead era.

Earliest commercial vessel on the lake was the *U.S. Grant* which first appeared as a sailboat in 1883 and was later converted to steam.

The *Pocahontas* was victimized by Flathead Lake's unpredictability in September 1887 while on a routine freight and passenger run between Foot of the Lake and Demersville on the Flathead River, north of the lake.

A violent windstorm struck as the ship cleared the Narrows. Waves crashed over the deck and high winds buffeted the sternwheeler as the skipper fought for control. He managed to guide the craft toward Idylwilde Island, off the west shore.

Just as calmer waters seemed within reach, jagged rocks suddenly loomed ahead and the *Pocahontas* plowed into them, took on water and sank. Fortunately she had grounded in a shallow channel. The only woman aboard and her child were placed in a lifeboat and reached land safely. All the men aboard swam to shore. Mail sacks and freight floated to shore and most of the cargo was recovered later.

The second half of the steamboat era started with the development of the townsite of Polson in 1909 and the beginning of homesteading in 1910.

Despite fierce competition, rival captains and their vessels unhesitatingly helped each other in emergencies. *The Lake Shore Sentinel* in its Dec. 10, 1909, issue told of an incident involving two boats southbound from Somers to Polson – the *Flyer* and the tugboat *Queen.*

Unable to punch through the ice in Polson Bay, the *Flyer* turned around and started back to Somers. The newspaper reported: *When the captain of the Flyer sighted the Queen, he asked permission to transfer his passengers to that boat and Captain Reed, thinking the Queen should be able to make its way through the ice, took on the Polson passengers. The Queen made good headway through the ice for ...perhaps two miles south of the Narrows, when it was discovered that a hole had been driven in her hull as a result of the heavy pounding she had received from the ice...*

The skipper headed toward shore but about 40 feet from land, the ship, its engine fires extinguished by water, settled to the bottom. The water was shallow and all passengers reached shore safely. The captain carried to safety two women passengers.

After reaching shore, word was sent to the nearest farmhouse and a team was hitched up to carry the cold and hungry travelers to the ferry landing opposite the city (Polson)...Their train of hard luck did not cease upon leaving the barge as one of the horses attached to the wagon dropped dead shortly after he was put in harness.

The *City of Polson* was involved in a scary incident in August 1910 when smoke from forest fires settled over Polson Bay. As the 61-ft. gasoline-powered ship approached Polson, visibility was reduced to zero. All hands groped in vain for sight of land.

Capt. J. W. Swanson ordered the boat stopped as he whistled for assistance. On shore, about a mile away, the operator of Polson's electric plant heard the whistle and recognized the problem. He sounded the power plant's whistle in reply. That helped Swanson get a bearing on land, but he still couldn't find the dock. After hitting a sand bar on the west side of the bay, he backed off, and then inched the boat slowly back toward the power plant signal until he finally found the landing.

The anticipation of the arrival of steamboats in the spring is reflected in diary entries by Polson area homesteader Lulu May Mansur:

March 21 -- All of Polson was excited over the fact that the steamer Montana was trying to make its way through the ice to Polson, but it failed and had to turn back.

March 24 -- ...The steamer Klondike made its first trip into Polson yesterday and the wind of last night took all of the ice out of the bay. It looked so good to see the boat steaming across to Polson after several months of rest because of the ice-blocked bay.

In 1915 more than 20 boats were operating with a combined capacity of 1,023 passengers and 900 tons of freight.

But the era was closing down by the early 1920s due to improved rail service and roads, more cars, buses and trucks, and a decline in homesteading. The *Kalispell* and the *Skincoots* were the last steamer and gasoline launch, respectively, to operate regularly scheduled passenger and freight runs. By 1927 the steamboat era was over although the third version of the *Klondike* took excursions as late as 1932.

A number of logging tugs including *Paul Bunyan, Reliance, Willis, Defiance, Dewey* and others continued to work for several years towing logs to mills. The *Paul Bunyan* is the sole surviving tug and is displayed outside the Miracle of America Museum on US 93, just south of Polson.

Flathead Fleet in fancy's flight

In 1968 while researching Flathead Lake's steamboat era, we made up this imaginary tale. Must've had a little too much time on our hands that week, but it was fun to watch it unfold on the typewriter! We've added a few more names of lake ships that we learned about later.

* * *

There's an old legend on Flathead Lake that says when oldtimers get together to hash over memories of the steamboating days, they once again can see the Flathead Fleet in fancy's flight: The bright yellow moon scales the snowcapped Missions, a brisk north wind whips up creamy caps on the shimmering black waters – and the stage is set. Soon the stately armada will pass in review.

Listen! The north wind carries sounds and voices from up around Somers, the steamboat center. Sounds almost like a circus, but it isn't. Those are steamboat skippers trying to drown out each other as through megaphones they shout "Hop aboard, folks. This craft is the fastest thing afloat" … "Ride the *Eva B*, the sleekest, speediest ship on the Flathead" … "Ours is the safest, plushest boats" … "Dine and drink your favorites as you sail along Flathead's shores" … "All aboard … We're bound for the Foot of the Lake" (Polson).

And here they come! Leading the fleet is the *U.S. Grant,* sailing just as proudly and as well as she did from 1874 to '76 when she carried passengers and the U.S. Mail with Capt. J.C. Kerr at the helm.

What's that gosh-awful whistlin' noise? Yep, it's the *Tom Carter*, steamboat 'round the bend. At the helm is the steady hand of Skipper Steve LeNeau, making the runs from 1888 to'92

Here's a white ghost steaming along the midnight waters, a clankin' and splashin' as she goes. A big 'un, the *Crescent,"* all 163 feet of her. At the wheel is sharp-eyed Captain Harry DePuy.

Another one? A twin? Not quite, but a steamboat that big and that long can only mean one thing. It's the *State of Montana* with its skippers Kerr and Cheney.

Do you hear a big brass band? It's none other than the old Klondike with big Gene Hodge at the wheel and a full party aboard, sailing full steam ahead past Wild Horse Island.

And here comes a different looking ship … looks like something built on the installment plan. Skipper's cabin on the bow, freight space amidship, boiler housing aft. It's the *Bigfork,* different but dependable under the commands of Captains Alfred Anderson, Harry Clubb, Chris Holand and Ernie von Euen.

Say! Look at that little craft go streaking by in front of the fleet … It's the *Eva B.* heading out to rescue a stranded float plane flyer named Maroney.

Here come the powerful little tugs. There's the *Paul Bunyan* with Angus MacDonald at the helm, and the *Queen* with Ben and Bill Cramer and the versatile von Euen doing the honors. And more tugs – *Reliance, Defiance, Willis,* and the *Dewey.* Where would the lumber mills be without 'em?

The parade goes on for hours. There go the *Wasco,* the *Flyer, Skincoots, Silver City,* the *Montana,* the *Pocahontas,* the *Demersville,* the *City of Polson,* the *Mary Lou, Mary Ann, Foot of the Lake Ferry, Bonita, Jim Hill, Helena, Star, t*he *Swan. Cassie D, Dolphin, Kalispell, Comet, Lillian, Dora,* and even the booze boat, the *Pastime,* used for a short time in 1915, to evade the prohibition laws on the Flathead Reservation. They're all there, every one of them.

But wait, hold everything. The moon has silently traveled to yon horizon, the wind has calmed, the star-flecked sky is turning gray. The ships and noises are fast fading. They've made port safely. The oldtimers are tired now. It's been rough work piloting the Flathead Fleet safely down the lake through tricky channels, shallows and narrows to the Port of Yesteryear in the land of Memory Lane. A well-deserved rest is at hand.

Ill-fated River Boat

The saga of the steamboat *City of Dixon* is a classic example of high hopes and bitter disappointments that marked the early homestead days on the Flathead Indian Reservation in western Montana. The steamboat's name reflected Dixon's municipal role as "The Gateway to the Flathead Reservation." Initial plans for the venture were announced in early April 1912 by the *Dixon Herald* and reprinted in the April 12, 1912, edition of the *Flathead Courier* of Polson.

Promoters were three Missoula men – Captain D.M. Roberts, veteran steamboat man who would serve as skipper of the river boat; Frank M. Pearson, a real estate and insurance man; and L.C. Bolton, an attorney.

The original plan was to build a 70-ft. long freight and excursion boat with a 16-ft. beam that would draw only 14 inches of water when loaded at 25-ton capacity. Powered by a 65 hp boiler and using a pair of 10x48 stern paddlewheel engines, she should run between Dixon and Sloan's Ferry, west of Ronan, on Flathead River.

The ill-fated river boat, City of Dixon.

The *Dixon Herald* editor predicted it would haul "over 200,000 bushels of grain, besides other material in the way of hay, lumber and merchandise; to be hauled this coming season ... It would also furnish the people of the Moiese Valley with a splendid means of transportation.

"This project is not going to interfere in the least with the already proposed electric road running from Dixon to Polson nor with the ferry road which is being built to tap the interior of the country on the west side of the river, and with these three means of transportation into Dixon, together with the main line of the N.P. railroad and the wagon roads already in good shape running into the town, we will begin to realize more fully the [Gateway] name given to Dixon."

The Dixon Transportation Company hoped to have the flagship sailing by July 1, 1912, but Murphy's Law was as alive and well in 1912 as it is today. Initial cost estimate was put at $7,000 but it ended up costing $12,000.

Plans changed early on as July 1 came and went and the boat had yet to be built. However, the anticipated route had been expanded to include 26 boat landings between Dixon and "the falls" [where Kerr Dam is now located}, a distance of 39 and a half river miles.

The order for construction was placed in late June with George Supple, a Portland, Oregon, shipbuilder. Machinery was ordered from Gillette, Eaton and Company of Lake City, Minnesota. Promoters planned to build the cabin in Dixon and then changed their minds and had Suppple do it. Work progressed fairly rapidly and the hull and cabin were shipped from Portland. By August 23, the disassembled material for the craft had arrived in Dixon by rail and was hauled to the river where a dock and a steaming vat had been built. Assembly began.

Launching was held Sunday, September 22. There had been rumors that a bottle of beer instead of champagne would have to be used to launch the craft because of liquor prohibitions on the reservation. But the real thing was used. The *Flathead Courier's* September 27 edition described the event:

"The largest crowd ever gathered at Dixon was in attendance at the launching ... They had band music, speech making and all the other things that are necessary for a real launching. Miss Chrissy Donlan of Missoula performed the christening act and as the boat slid into the water broke a 'sure enough' bottle of champagne across the prow."

The ship's vital statistics had changed from the original plan. Now the *City of Dixon* was 80 feet long, and 20 feet wide with a draft of 15 inches of water when loaded. The engine was rated 60 horsepower. The *Courier* reported, "It is expected to make one round trip daily from Dixon to a point a short distance before the tunnel camp … It's claimed that the up trip will take about five hours and the down three. If the boat proves to be able to buck the rapids successfully it will be a big thing to the settlers on both sides of the river, as it will give them an opportunity to market their grain and other produce without costing so much and taking so much time to deliver. It will be some time yet before the boat will be ready for service."

A short shakedown cruise was made Thanksgiving afternoon. The *Dixon Herald* reported, "Captain Roberts gave Chief Engineer Meikle the bells and with a slam of the lever, the sound of steam and the splash of the paddle wheel the steamer *City of Dixon* swung free from the shore and backed out into the stream. Swinging around she headed upstream and made her way against the current at a rapid rate. The engines were new and everything worked more or less at a disadvantage but considering all things, the first trial was encouraging … Aside from a little fixing and re-adjusting about the machinery she is all right and the *City of Dixon* will soon be in shape to make regular trips on the Flathead River."

Apparently it took more than just a little fixing – all of 1913 and half of 1914 to be exact. Finally, during the last half of June 1914, the ship made her maiden voyage. Scheduled to leave at 10:30 a.m. the departure was delayed by the late arrival of Northern Pacific train No. 41 from Missoula, which carried a large number of boat passengers. Some people complained that there were so many Missoulians wanting a ride that there might not be enough room for the locals.

The *Herald* editor wrote, "… Missoula was there and in fact was better represented, considering the proportion of those interested in the boat, than was Dixon … The first stop was made at the Indian Agency, where some more passengers were taken on board, and from there no more halts were made until the boat had gone about ten miles where she landed at a small island, stopping about an hour for a picnic dinner."

The Dixon newspaper story devoted several inches to an account of a mother duck and her two ducklings trying – successfully – to dodge the oncoming "huge water monster" as it raced downstream. The boat arrived in Dixon just in time for the Missoulians to catch Train No. 42 for home.

There is no mention of any more trips being made but probably a few sailings were accomplished. The August 14, 1914, *Flathead Courier* reported, "The *City of Dixon*, a steamboat plying on the Flathead River, was struck by lightning early Friday and burned to the water's edge … The boat was lying at its moorings on the waterfront when the bolt struck it, but the fire burned the hawsers and the craft drifted downstream until it lodged against the cables of the Indian ferry some distance below the town. Holes were burned in the bottom, it was reported, and the boat is slowly filling.

"The *City of Dixon* was built by Dixon people as a carrier of produce from the rich farm lands in the reservation country. Its whole history was marked by disasters, the last of which seems to have ended the whole tale." That prediction was validated when it was announced that insurance coverage totaled only $44,000.

The MS Flathead led the boat parade off Boettcher Park during Polson's 1960 Golden Jubilee celebration.

Last of the old-time tour boats

The MS Flathead originally was the Glacier National Park tour boat, St. Mary. It was purchased by Stan Koss and brought to Polson, retrofitted and renamed the MS Flathead. At the beginning of the summer tourist season on Flathead Lake, the Polson Chamber of Commerce sponsored a "goodwill tour" of lakeshore communities. Chamber members would go ashore and visit with local business people and exchange plans for the coming visitor season. In 1961, the day before the goodwill tour, Skipper Koss took the ship out for a test run. A fuel line broke and the resulting fire destroyed the craft. Here, Koss poles the burned hulk to its final resting place, now the site of KwaTaqNuk Resort.

Paul Fugleberg photos

History rides the wind in Bannack

History rides the wind in the ghost town of Bannack, Montana's first territorial capital. It whispers through trees, moans in and around the empty buildings. You can taste it in the dust devils swirling up from the dirt street that once teemed with miners, merchants, freighters, dance hall dollies, Chinese cooks and launderers, territorial politicians, road agents and drifters.

Never an ordinary territorial capital or mining camp, Bannack always was different. It still is. Today, it's the only ghost town incorporated into Montana's state parks system.

Amazingly, Bannack appears much as it did in pioneer days – no telephone or power wires and poles, no modern homes, offices or commercial establishments, no paved streets. Of more than 200 original buildings, nearly 90 are still standing.

From the dusty main street and creek bottoms to the tip of nearby hills, what you see is about what the miners saw – with the exception, of course, of what aging, erosion and foliage growth have contributed.

Visitors should allow at least two or three hours to appreciate the Bannack experience. That gives them time to shift the imagination into gear and absorb the atmosphere.

Although there were less than a thousand inhabitants when it was named territorial capital, the population swelled to some 5,000 when gold mining in nearby Grasshopper Creek was at its peak. The boom brought in influx of all types of humans – good and bad, dedicated and misguided, ambitious and ne'er-do-wells.

Helping to recapture some of those moments is a self-guided walking tour that permits interior inspection of many structures. With a minimum of effort visitors can visualize some of the camp's colorful incidents.

Handsome, educated, conniving Henry Plummer came to town on Christmas Day, 1862. A short time later he mortally wounded Jack Cleveland, an old outlaw friend, and then went hunting for Sheriff Hank Crawford, just in case Cleveland had made a deathbed statement.

Forewarned, Crawford made a preemptive strike with a rifle shot and broke Plummer's arm. Before Plummer could regain his shooting prowess, Crawford left for Wisconsin and Plummer was elected Sheriff of both Bannack and Virginia City.

Plummer had two jails built in Bannack. They still stand with their barred windows, thick log walls and sod roofs. But terror still reigned along the 90-mile stretch of road from Bannack to Virginia City. Headed surreptitiously by Sheriff Plummer, ruthless road agents allegedly murdered some 102 travelers, robbed countless others, and waylaid stages at will.

Vigilantes finally ferreted out Plummer and his gang, "The Innocents " – Boone Helm, Cyrus Skinner, George Shears, Whiskey Bill Graves, George Ives, Red Yeager, Buck Stinson and Ned Ray. Captured in his Bannack home, Plummer groveled and pleaded with the Vigilantes to cut off his ears, turn him out naked in the snow – anything but hanging. Finally, he faced the inevitable and told his captors, "Give me a clean drop."

Another tragic Bannack chapter involved an Illinois girl, Helen Patterson. At 16 years of age, she promised Howard Humphrey she'd marry him, but first she wanted to go out west with a sister and brother-in-law.

Once she got to Bannack, she forgot poor Howard, She assumed the name Nellie Paget, became a dance hall hostess, and was caught up in the wild life of the mining camp – until at 22, she was shot dead by an enraged suitor in a saloon.

But that wasn't the end of the story. Howard Humphrey learning of the tragedy, refused to believe it. After waiting 55 years for her return to Illinois, he went to Montana to find her. He located her – in the sagebrush-dotted Bannack cemetery.

A more joyous occasion occurred when the colorful Methodist frontier circuit rider, W.W. (Brother Van) Van Orsdel, came to town. Brother Van preached, taught and sang to the people of Bannack as he personally directed the construction of a Methodist church. He had a lot of extra helpers because townspeople feared an imminent Indian attack on the community. The church today is still used for occasional worship services.

After the battle of the Big Hole on Aug. 8, 1877, members of Chief Joseph's band of Nez Perce camped on Horse Prairie Creek near Bannack. Hillsides were fortified and women and children were housed in the new county courthouse, but an attack never came.

Bannack, which sprouted after Montana's first major gold discovery occurred along Grasshopper Creek in 1862, was named by George Washington Stapleton and was spelled Bannack to differentiate it from Bannock, a settlement near Boise City. Another theory is that the spelling originated from a typographical error.

Actually both Bannack and Bannock were in Idaho Territory at the time. Montana didn't achieve territorial status until 1864. Territorial Governor Sidney Edgerton proclaimed Bannack as the capital and the first legislature met there in 1864-65.

But Bannack's political tenure was brief. In 1865 with gold reserves dwindling and the population decreasing the legislature voted to move the capital to more prosperous Virginia City. Yet Bannack didn't dry up and blow away. A Masonic hall-school building was constructed in 1874. A year later, a two-story county courthouse was completed and the Methodist church was built in 1877.

The courthouse, which later became the Meade Hotel, is one of the most impressive buildings in Bannack. It served as the county courthouse for only six years because the county seat was moved to Dillon in 1881 after the arrival of the railroad.

Around 1890, Dr. Christian Meade converted the red brick structure into the hotel and community social center. In the large dining room were several tables, each topped with spotless white tablecloths. The hotel operated until 1940.

Among other buildings still standing are the drug store and assay office; the Jackson home, whose owners operated the Goodrich Hotel and a general store; Skinner's Saloon; a few relics on Bachelors' Row; the Graves House, the first frame home in the territory; the Renois log cabin, one of the oldest in Bannack; Amede (Misty) Bessette's cabin, which provided its owner shelter until his death in 1919; George Chrisman's store, now used as a warehouse; the Gibson boarding houses, one of which served as a blacksmith shop, and Dr. Rayburn's home.

Ghosts of Henry Plummer's highwaymen rode briefly on Nov. 4, 1931, when two masked, armed robbers held up five persons and the bartender at Monte Verdick's bar (soft drinks only – Prohibition era, you know) and got off with $800. The Associated Press wire story commented, "Only the escape lacked historic color. They roared out of town in a powerful car…"

The old ghost town booms back to life each July as visitors and local folks celebrate Bannack Days. Frontier crafts, music and drama are featured along with a black powder muzzle-loader shoot, Sunday church services, horse and buggy and antique truck rides and more. Annual Halloween events are also scheduled.

Bannack State Park, 25 miles west-southwest of Dillon and about 30 miles southeast of Jackson, is easily reached by a well-maintained four-mile gravel road leading south from Montana Highway 278.S

Left, this building served as the county courthouse from 1875 to 1881. In 1890, it became the Meade Hotel which operated until 1940. Above, these are the gallows from which Sheriff Henry Plummer and his cronies stepped off into eternity.

Paul Fugleberg photos

An unhappy beginning

The Hell Gate Treaty of 1855 established the Flathead Indian Reservation with headquarters in the Jocko Valley near present day Arlee. However many Indians remained in the Bitterroot Valley despite the abandonment of St. Mary's mission.

On November 14, 1871, President U.S. Grant issued an executive order to relocate the Salish to the reservation. Some of them moved in 1873, but one band of 360, headed by Chief Charlot, refused to go.

The years were not kind. White settlers moved into the Bitterroot Valley and the Indians' living conditions gradually deteriorated. Finally, in 1885, through the influence of Indian Agent Peter Ronan, the government distributed wagons, horses and plows to the Bitterroot band to help them in farming efforts. But it was too little, too late.

Chief Charlot was justifiably bitter. He had refused to sign the Garfield Agreement in 1872 which provided for the relocation of the Indians to the Jocko Valley as well as allotting 160-acre tracts to those remaining in the Bitterroot. Charlot and other tribal members had no faith in the federal pledges because the government had failed to keep its Hell Gate Treaty promises to send carpenters, blacksmiths, artisans and teachers. And no survey had been made yet of the Bitterroot lands to see if they would be more suitable for the Indians.

Adding insult to injury, General James A. Garfield, later president of the United States – reported that Charlot had signed the agreement to move. He had not signed. The original document bore out Charlot's claim. Garfield had assumed the chief would sign when he saw the provisions were kept, thus he reported that Charlot had agreed.

Citing the destitute conditions, Charlot in 1891 reluctantly and poignantly announced, "I will go – I and my children. My young men are becoming bad, they have no place to hunt. My women are hungry. For their sake, I will go. I do not want the land you promise. I do not believe your promises. All I want is enough ground for my grave. We will go over there."

Nature on a rampage

Madison Canyon Earthquake

What were you doing shortly before midnight on August 17, 1959?

Of course, a lot of you weren't even on Earth yet. But those who were living in western Montana at that time remember. We were just going to bed when my wife said, "We're having an earthquake."

"Naw, I don't feel anything," I said plopping my head onto the pillow.

"Look at the clothes in the closet. They're swaying."

"Well, it's probably the breeze blowing through the window."

"There's no wind blowing."

By then I had zonked out – it had been a long day.

When I went up town in the morning, I learned she was right. There had been an earthquake – the historic Madison Canyon quake near Hebgen Lake, a few miles from the northwest corner of Yellowstone National Park.

And I had missed it! I quickly learned more.

***

A full, bright yellow moon – as yet untouched by man's feet – sailed silently through the summer sky over the Madison River Canyon on August 17, Most of the campers in Rock Creek Campground had settled down, many anticipating early morning forays against the fighting trout in the nearby blue ribbon Madison River.

In the pre-midnight calm only the slightest noises were heard. Mosquitoes buzzed, a dog barked, a coyote yipped, occasionally a car hummed along the highway. The sounds blended with the Madison's melody to produce a camper's lullaby.

Peaceful. Until 11:37 p.m. when a cataclysmic quake, registering 7.1 on the Richter scale, shattered the stillness. In a matter of minutes lives and landscapes were changed forever.

A chain reaction occurred; chunks of earth dropped, others rose; boulders bounded downward; Hebgen Lake tilted; seiches sloshed over earth-filled Hebgen Dam three times and roared down the Madison River; highways heaved; trees toppled; buildings buckled; a mountain moved – 80 million tons of it in 20 seconds to form a huge natural dam and create Earthquake Lake. An instant cemetery was created at Rock Creek Campground. At least 19 persons were buried as slide debris covered the campground. All told, 28 persons died in quake, scores of others were injured.

Campers and canyon residents who were sleeping when the quake struck awoke to a real life nightmare that continued for many hours.

Today, the Madison Canyon Slide Area provides a graphic lesson in practical geology and is a major tourist attraction. In the comfortable visitor center, naturalists explain precisely what happened that night and why.

Dave Infausto of Hillsboro, Oregon, views the mammoth Madison Canyon slide.

(Paul Fugleberg photo)

Quake-damaged cabin is still an exhibit on Hebgen Lake, but visitors can't get inside now. When this picture was taken shortly after the event, there was no prohibition yet against photographing from the inside.

Paul Fugleberg photo

Charts and maps indicate that one of the strongest earthquakes ever recorded in the continental United States rumbled upward and outward from its epicenter, eight to ten miles beneath the surface in Red Canyon, not far from the eastern end of the Madison River Canyon. The shock waves caused tremendous displacement along the old Hebgen and Red Canyon faults.

The site is fascinating, but there's still an eeriness to the night along Quake Lake shores – especially on moonless nights and during late night summer storms when the gray ghost trees dance in gusty winds to the beat of thunder drums and strobe-like lightning flashes.

Quake Lake's ghost trees are silhouetted at sundown   Paul Fugleberg photo

Mount St. Helens
Neither saint nor lady

Sunday morning about 8 a.m., May 18, 1980, in a matter of seconds, the magnificent landscape around Mount St. Helens in southwestern Washington was changed forever. For weeks the volcano had been threatening a major eruption and it finally happened – an explosive lateral eruption, big time.

As the top and large portion of the north face of the mountain disappeared in a horrifying cloud of ash, the shock wave roared through the area at 300 miles per hour. You would think that the blast wave would have traveled in a straight line, leaving leeward slopes and lower places untouched. Not this blast. It went up and down mountain slopes, ridges, coulees, nooks and crannies – toppling, sandblasting, and scorching everything in its path. Then it baked it under 450-degree layer of volcanic ash.

Sixty-two people died.

Mount St. Helens destruction reached out to areas untouched by the blast wave, too. Racing down the slopes at speeds of up to 60 miles per hour, hot mud flows and pyroclastic lava topped trees, carried away cabins, demolished bridges, choked rivers and streams. The depth of the flows is easily seen from mud marks on trees and snags in downstream valleys.

The fallout pattern of the ash spread rapidly eastward. Ritzville, Yakima, Spokane and other communities experienced what they termed "Ash Sunday" as countless tons of ash fell. Commerce as far away as Polson, Ronan, St. Ignatius and Missoula, Montana, had to be shut down for a couple days due to the choking, penetrat-

Looking into crater from Windy Ridge area viewpoint.   Paul Fugleberg photo

ting ash.

In the days preceding the eruption, I had begun planning to visit my uncle in Vancouver, Washington, hoping I could be closer to the action. But Mount St. Helens, neither saint nor lady, beat me to it, visiting Polson in the form of falling ash that by Monday morning had covered the area to give the impression that everything was blanketed by powdered dry cement.

Within a few weeks I did make that trip to Vancouver, but of course it was impossible to visit the blast zone. We did inspect the devastation on the downriver side. I'll admit I was glad I wasn't there for the main event.

It was four years before I could return there. And the experience was memorable and shocking. The silence under the sweltering mid-summer sun was staggering. No birds were chirping or singing, no bees buzzing, no flies humming or mosquitoes zinging. Not even a whisper of wind. The only sound was my footsteps as they padded through the dusty ash. It was like walking through the "Day after" – but this was more than four years after.

The scene was that of a valley of death – almost. Gnarled ghost trees bent eerily. Others raised scorched, bare, limbless trunks skyward in defiance of nature's power. Thousands more, like gigantic toothpicks, were scattered grotesquely in all directors. Reflecting it was tiny Meta Lake in the heart of the Mount St. Helens National Volcanic Monument blast zone.

Barren, devastated and devoid of the area's once majestic beauty, we noted signs of life re-emerging. Brilliant green clumps of brush and small trees were forcing their way upward. In time – perhaps a lot of time – they should prevail. Life inexorably goes on.

* * *

Ruth Forssen and her husband, the late John Forssen, had an unplanned encounter with Mount St. Helens en route home from a visit with their son and daughter-in-law in Port Townsend, Washington, May 18 and 19.

Pat Paro, the *Flathead Courier's* Dayton-Proctor correspondent, wrote about it in the *Courier*. Here's a condensation of Pat's report:

They left Port Townsend on the 8:30 ferry. Crossing Snowqualmie Pass, Ruth began to doze and John turned on the car radio to keep her awake.

They were soon both awake when they heard that Mount St. Helens had erupted. As they descended the east side of the pass, they began to see dust in the air, and soon Washington highway patrolmen blocked the Interstate 90 and directed them north to Wenatchee and US Highway 2.

Turning east at Wenatchee on US 2, they came to thicker and thicker dust, with traffic raising blinding clouds that sometimes made it necessary to stop completely. Soon after they passed Waterfield, the road was closed. A few miles ahead, at Wilbur, more dust-masked officers were encountered and told them they could go no farther. But after an hour, traffic was allowed to proceed, with Ruth, John, their car and all their trappings, including some fine Pacific Ocean driftwood and shells, becoming coated with a thicker and thicker coating of Mount St. Helens.

* * *

including some fine Pacific Ocean driftwood and shells, becoming coated with a thicker and thicker coating of Mount St. Helens.

At Davenport the half-dark turned all dark and they were stopped again, along with a hundred or so other travelers. The procession stood motionless in the main street of Davenport for an hour or so. Then the police let one car go every two minutes to minimize the problem of swirling dust. Ruth and John and the others proceeded along Main Street, 30 feet at a time, and two hours later they were on their way to Spokane.

Determined to drive all night if necessary to get home, they plowed through the dusty night. But at 11 p.m. in Spokane, the atmosphere was thick enough to cut with a knife, and they gave up and sought out a motel, taking baths which must have come close to clogging the drains.

The next morning John dumped a cup of Mount St. Helens out of the car's air filter and they went off, ignoring radio and TV pleadings that all roads out of Spokane were closed to all traffic. Traffic was light and the dust became lighter except for a quite thick pocket in the Plains area.

Proceeding directly to Polson they picked up their cat, Pizzicato, and dog, Waggy, at the veterinarian's and then headed home, the cat throwing up along the way.

All in all, the Forssens reported that they had never been so glad to see their little gray home on the west shore.

Unusual incidents

Trouble over Bridged Waters

Bridges aren't always connecting links. Sometimes they've been known to create wide gaps among the citizenry. It happened in Polson during the summer of 1910.

Homesteaders and city residents looked forward to completion of the new city's first bridge across the Pend Oreille [now the Flathead] River connecting west shore communities with Polson.

Original plans called for a single approach on both sides of the river with Flathead County putting up $7,100 and local people providing the balance of funding as well as contributing labor on the approaches.

Construction of the 1,842-ft. long, 16-ft. wide bridge began in June. The trouble started when merchants began arguing about the approach on the Polson side of the river -- whether it should connect with B Street or C Street Ultimately a "Y"-shaped, twin approach was constructed which connected both streets to the bridge...but only after a huge hassle.

The Burrill Bridge Company's construction engineer R. W. Sweet and foreman John Gore soon found themselves in the middle of a major dispute.

Tempers reached the boiling point in mid-August when work on the C Street approach was halted by an injunction filed by B Street proponents.

The majority on the city council, however, favored C Street and responded by agreeing to allow B Street to be graded as soon as the C Street approach was done. This aroused the ire of the B Streeters, who began grading the street without a permit the next morning.

The *Flathead Courier* reported: *Two men were put to work, but the mayor soon hove in sight and told them to quit. They failed to obey his orders so they were arrested and the work stopped until that evening when four men started in to grade. They were almost immediately arrested but later released.*

The men evidently thought the mayor didn't mean it for they returned to work. Chief of Police Hern . . . gathered them in, escorted them to the jail, and locked them up for the night.

The next morning the mayor put up a sign closing B Street. Bridge Engineer Sweet nailed up a barricade to the bridge. A man working for the C Street people fixing a temporary approach was arrested. The C's retaliated by pinching another B Street workman who was charged with cutting a tree in the park.

Some west side ranchers tore down Sweet's barricade and crossed on the bridge without looking at the "no trespass" signs.

Meanwhile, Salish and Kootenai Indians who had seldom had any difficulty crossing the river before the bridge, watched stoically from the sidelines.

At this point Sheriff O'Connell came down from Kalispell and things quieted down a trifle.

A C Street delegation took the noon boat to Somers and went overland to Kalispell and obtained an injunction tying up the entire project.

The *Courier* editor commented: *With eight men under arrest, two injunction suits, every attorney in Polson employed, police and justice court working overtime, special officers being sworn in, everybody talking writs, the code, and how stubborn the other fellow was, it began to look like pickings for news.*

But now it is all over, the injunction suits have been withdrawn, the arrested men turned loose, the lawyers have gone fishing, the mayor is rusticating in the hills, the sheriff and commissioners have come and gone, the bridge is completed and will soon have two approaches, and everybody loves his neighbor no matter on which street he lives.

The bridge and its twin approaches served Polson until being replaced with a single approach, piling span that was built in 1927. The present concrete bridge was completed in 1966 and updated in 2009.

Considerably more expensive and difficult to build, but with much less controversy than Polson's first bridge, is the Lake Koocanusa Bridge near Eureka. The bridge is the highest (247 feet above minimum lake level) and longest (2,437 feet) in Montana. It cost $9 million; construction started in June 1967 and was completed in September 1971. The lake was formed by completion of Libby Dam and covered the town of Rexford, which was moved to higher ground.

Those magnificent mowing machines

I've gone through a few generations of lawn mowers since I was a kid in the Hollywood Hills, pushing a reel-type mower on steel wheels up and down neighborhood streets to mowing jobs to earn a buck or two. No one had big lawns in that steep-walled canyon. It took longer to get to some of the jobs than to do the actual mowing.

During high school summers I'd work on my aunt's farm near Clark, South Dakota. One of my tasks was to keep the yard mowed with a home-built electric mower on which the blade extended at least three inches beyond the engine platform. One day I got my foot a little too close and the blade zipped across the top of the work boot's toe. Feeling no pain, I was still apprehensive as I unlaced the boot, took it off and discovered the top of my sock was also slit. Took the sock off, looked down and discovered my toes were unscathed. Uff da! What a relief!

Fast forward to February 1959, after moving to Polson and renting the house that is now Pat DeVries' CPA office, next to the Uptown Apartments. Rent was $40 a month. An old power mower was on the property and we agreed to mow the lawn. Then in December, we purchased our own house on 12th Avenue East. That meant buying our own mower, and several more after that.

Invariably each rattlin', vibratin', teeth jarrin' machine was pushed by a wheezin', snortin', sneezin', spittin' pusher -- me. Until the kids were old enough to do the job. When the empty nest syndrome inflicted its impact, I wasn't looking forward to the asthmatic ordeal, but high schooler Aaron Schalk came looking for mowing jobs. He did a great job – and still does years after completing high school and college.

Several years ago, I loaned my mower to someone – I've forgotten who – and it hasn't shown up since. Thank goodness!

But whatever problems I had with those magnificent mowing machines paled in comparison to those of Montana's first electric mowing machine operator. George W. Gregson operated a health spa and hotel near Butte and he claimed to have invented the world's first electric lawn mower in 1885.

It was a horse-drawn mowing machine with an 85-pound attachment that generated electricity. The juice heated a metallic ribbon that burned off the grass close to the ground. At least that was the theory.

Gregson invited a Butte reporter, a Mr. Schussler, to the hot springs to witness a demonstration of his innovative mowing machine. The inventor filled the batteries with "bluestone and acid" and hitched the horses to the cutter. Then Schussler persuaded Gregson to let him make the historic initial run. Schussler climbed aboard, took the reins and put the horses and machine into action. It worked beautifully. Grass cascaded behind the mower in a bright green shower.

The inventor beamed with pride. Surely that machine would make a noteworthy contribution to agriculture – and bring a meaningful monetary return, too. But the euphoria was brief. Suddenly, according to press reports, "Schussler rose from his seat and turned a backward somersault, following the shower of grass." The horses spooked, smashing the mower into pieces against the side of the hotel.

Inspection revealed that apparently Schussler had driven the horses too fast, which generated too much electricity. The current found its way through the iron seat on which driver was perched. It was at that point that Schussler and the machine parted company via the spectacular backward flip.

Gregson commented that there were a few imperfections to work out. He felt that by composing the seat of a "non-conductor material," he could "keep the driver from getting overheated."

Apparently he never followed through with the improvements.

Al Thiri had to do a bit of climbing to get this "aerial view" of Sperry Glacier in Glacier National Park in the mid-19-teens.

Colorful personalities

Danger was Al Thiri's companion

There were two things for certain about Al Thiri, early day western Montana photographer.

1. Danger was his constant companion.
2. He often seemed to be "up in the air" over one thing or another.

Literally.

In Polson, Montana, in 1910, for instance, local residents claimed they could usually tell a stranger in town when Thiri was at work. The newcomer might be gawking skyward, mouth agape, sometimes breathless. Local folks, however, would rarely glance up. They knew it was just Al Thiri doing what he did best – taking his "aerial view" pictures, hanging out of an upper story window, teetering on the edge or a roof, strapped onto a telephone pole, perched in a tree or peering down from high atop a grain elevator. While he operated in the shadows of the artistic talents of Herman Schnitzmeyer, R.M. McKay and T.J. Hileman, the most noted area photographers the homestead era, Thiri's pictures had a unique perspective. That's why he called his business "Thiri's Aerial View Service."

He had started taking aerial views in Minnesota in 1906 while employed by the St. Paul Souvenir Company. Many photographs marked "T.A.V.S." are still found in family photo albums in western Montana communities.

Actually Thiri was not his real name. He was born Albert Olsen in 1884 in Minnesota, but when he lived in St. Paul there were so many other Olsens that he frequently could not get his own mail at the post office. So he changed his handle to Thiri and kept it when he moved west even though his four brothers – Ole, Sam, Andrew and Lloyd – retained the Olsen name.

He came to Polson from Spokane, Washington, in May 1910. As early as June 1, 1910, shortly after the Flathead Indian Reservation was opened to homesteading, Thiri placed ads in Polson's first weekly newspaper, the *Lake Shore Sentinel,* and the new *Flathead Courier* weekly proclaiming "Thiri's Aerial Views are on sale at the drugstore and post office."

A month later, figuring that another form of high altitude work would be good for advertising his business, he featured himself as "Dare Devil Develo" during Polson's Fourth of July celebration and jumped from a 50-ft. high platform on the city docks through a hoop of fire into Flathead Lake. Windy weather delayed the jump until late in the day, but the *Courier* commented "All who saw the dive were satisfied as to the nerve of the diver."

A year later he performed at the Plains Fair as "Thiri, the Helldiver," leaping from the wagon bridge spanning the Clark's Fork River through a circle of flame. He also claimed that he would set a record by holding his breath under water for three and a half minutes. There was no follow-up story on whether or not he achieved the record.

In July 1910, the urge to take new views elsewhere in Montana found him moving around the Treasure State as a representative of the Cohn Brothers Postcard Jobbers of Butte. He moved to Chinook in September 1910 to work for Charles Morris, publisher of postcards, calendars and holiday goods.

Before he left Polson, though, he had a narrow escape while returning from a picture taking expedition to Camas Hot Springs and Dayton. The *Sentinel* reported, "Mr. Thiri walked in from Dayton and states that at a point near the Irvine ranch he was chased by a herd of buffalo (part of the Allard-Pablo herd). Ever alert for good views, Mr. Thiri set his tripod and frantically waved his coat to keep the beasts from charging, and secured a good picture of the buffalo. This story is hard to believe but Mr. Thiri has the film to prove it."

By the summer of 1911, he was back home in Polson photographing grain fields and threshing outfits. He operated from Polson for the next few years taking pictures of local homesteaders as well as in Big Arm, Elmo, Ronan, St. Ignatius and other reservation communities.

In May 1914 he looked into the possibilities of making some aerial views in Glacier National Park, but he was nearly grounded permanently. The *Flathead Courier* of Polson reported that he was trapped by avalanches near Sperry Glacier and lived for three days and nights on some Grape Nuts he had carried in with him.

In 1916 Thiri was ready to try his hand at something different. He became a first class ranger in Glacier National Park with headquarters at Belton (now West Glaciers). At the time the *Daily Inter Lake* of Kalispell reported, "Mr. Thiri is well known in this county and has many friends who will be glad to learn of his appointment. For a number of years he was located at Polson and his photographs of western life taken on the reservation achieved national fame."

His Glacier Park adventures were among his favorites. He expressed amazement at the agility of mountain goats and how they could get out of sight so quickly – so fast that the first time he encountered a goat he watched it with admiration and forgot to take the picture.

He told a *Seattle Times* reporter, "The hard part of mountain climbing is not the ascent but the descent." Flattened against a cliff, overhanging a drop of say 3,000 feet, Thiri said he could follow the goats and find footing wherever they went – while on the way up. But, the picture taken, the photographer faced his real danger on the trip down where one has to feel with the feet to find places to step.

Thiri traveled through most of the wild places alone. Most of the time he was unarmed and carried a limited supply of raisins, chocolates, cheese and Grape Nuts. He also took with him a small vest-pocket camera and film.

His Glacier Park experiences occurred before mass intrusion of the grizzly bear's domain. At that time he reported there was "absolutely no danger from wild animals in the woods." Even grizzlies, he said, held no terrors for one who knew the forest. He said he had passed within a few feet of them with only a stick for protection. By dragging the stick, he said, he was able to frighten away any grizzly.

When traveling by horseback, however, Thiri hung bells on the saddle because he felt grizzlies thought horses were deer. He told friends that he had lost horses to bears when he forgot to put on the bells. His camp was raided by a grizzly once. Leaving a pot of prunes to boil on the camp stove, Thiri was away from camp for just few minutes. When he returned he found that the bear apparently burned its paws, which enraged the animal. After wrecking the camp, the bear managed to drag away a case of canned goods about 150 yards before abandoning it. Thiri thought the animal's paws were burned too painfully to tote them any farther.

Neither cougars nor mountain lions were feared by Thiri. He said, "I have seen dozens of those and have learned to ignore them entirely. They won't attack unless cornered." He'd probably take a different view of that today as some cats' habits have changed as humans encroached upon their habitat.

The photographer never carried a compass in the woods. He said he found that compasses were no good in mountain country – too many minerals influence the needle. He determined directions mostly by stars or by trees. He said that at night the Big Dipper is a faithful guide. The two stars forming the outside of the cup always point to the North Star. "No stars, no sun, the trees or grass may always be depended upon," he claimed. Trees, he said, have few branches on the west side, and grass always lies toward the east.

He told a *Seattle Times* reporter, "Sometimes when I'm at the top of a mountain, I feel that surely I'm on the most desolate spot in the world. Nothing but rocks and snow on all sides with the blue sky above and clouds below, one wonders how it is possible for even a goat to live in such a place.

"'If one waits long enough, often he will see a goat nosing around through the snow. He will pick a stray piece of moss here and there or unearth some unseen herb. In times like these, the city and its high cost of living, with people grumbling about the price of ham and eggs seems far away. Goats live where seemingly there is nothing to live for, and they seem to be happy for the chance."

MID-WEEK-MARKET-SCENE
POLSON-FLATHEAD-RESERVATION-MONT.

Weather never dampened Thiri's spirit; it simply added to the challenge. In the winter of 1919 he started a ten-mile hike through a blizzard in sub-zero temperatures, according the *Seattle Sunday Times* account: "At the end of ten miles, where he had cached a food supply, he found upon arriving that his stores had been stolen. During the night he dare not go to sleep. At daybreak he started again for a 17-mile journey to a settlement. The snow was two feet deep. His hands were so numbed that he couldn't light a match when he stopped to build a fire. To get heat he put the match in his mouth and scratched his head against a small wood ax."

"This was the nearest I came to getting caught by Nature," he said. "I didn't dare sit down during the 17-mile hike. I knew that if I got off my feet, I wouldn't be able to get up. I rested by leaning against trees." Thiri commented that he wouldn't trade his profession for that of the President.

While in Washington he took pictures of Mount Rainier and other Cascades peaks as well as shinnying atop the L.S. Smith Building to photograph Seattle from that vantage point. He said "The Smith Building flagpole is a cinch. Some of these human flies ought to try mountain scaling. Any distance above 100 feet is all the same to me. A drop of 100 feet in the air means death. From that height up to 10,000 feet there is no difference."

Despite living on the ragged edge for so many years, the photographer became ill sometime in 1920. *Flathead Courier* items reported that he was incapacitated and that his mother, Mrs. A.H. Lunder of Polson, sought funds to send him to Rochester or someplace for specialized treatment. In August 1921, with the assistance of Dr. J.L. Richards, Dr. Witherspoon and Mrs. E. E. Dubois, all of Polson, he was able to enter the Butte hospital for treatment.

However, he couldn't be helped and he died May 1, 1923, at the age of 39, in Kalispell, Montana, in the home of Mrs. Alice Peterson. The body was returned to Polson where funeral services were held in Lakeview Cemetery. His grave is high on a hill affording a splendid "aerial view" of Flathead Lake.

Colonel White's Dreams

"Colonel" Almon A. White may have been the king of the dreamers in the Flathead Lake region of western Montana in the 19-teens and early '20s.

Example: He proposed two palatial auto ferries to run on a route connecting the Northern Pacific Railway in Polson, the Great Northern at Somers, the "Missoula and Flathead Electric Railway terminus on Finley Point" and Wild Horse Island. The ferries would carry 30 cars plus 1,000 passengers on the upper decks.

His Wild Horse Island development called for 14 miles of shoreline, 20 miles of saddle trails, a spacious hotel, natatorium, pavilion, extensive golf links, clubhouse, yacht club, anglers club, electric light and pumping plant, ferry steamer and pleasure docks, and Summit Park on the crest of the island.

It was all in the September 17, 1917, edition of the *Flathead Courier* in which the Civil War veteran outlined his plan to develop the largest island in Flathead Lake. Obviously, it never came about.

Colonel White burst onto the scene in flamboyant style in late July 1915 when 905 lots in 21 villa sites on the lower half of the lake were offered for sale at public auction by the federal government.

THE S.S. KLONDIKE ARRIVING AT POLSON, MONT
ON FLATHEAD LAKE

Colonel A.A. White had one of his offices near the Grandview Hotel, approximately where the present Salish Building is now. The early day developer never got his fancy stone and glass building.

He paid down $18,000 for the Wild Horse Island lots. He hoped to sell them for $40 to $100 per acre. Colonel White also bought other villa sites as well as some land from private owners. Some tracts he re-sold, but eventually many were lost when he failed to meet payment requirements and the government took the land back. Other lots that he couldn't re-sell were taken by the county for back taxes.

The term "low key" was not in the colonel's vocabulary. To transport prospective customers to villa sites, he operated the "White Auto and Launch" system between Flathead Lake and Glacier National Park. The system included four seven-passenger cars and several launches. Four boats were stationed on Flathead Lake, two on McDonald Lake in Glacier Park and one on Swan Lake. Drivers and launch captains were uniformed and two men in white uniforms were stationed in Glacier Park to inform tourists of the properties. There was no charge for the cruises or motor tours.

In September 1915 Colonel White brought his office furniture, launches and cars to Polson, obtained a 10-year lease on a pie-shaped piece of land and announced plans for a stone and glass building in which to display valley products and house the Chamber of Commerce. His office would be in a tent on the grounds. The structure was never built.

The next year Colonel White announced plans for a 50 ft. x 24 ft. bungalow style office building at B and Third Street [now U.S. 93 and Main Street] on the Grandview Hotel site. He also hired an engineer to survey a route for the "Missoula-Polson" electric railway, and had printed and distributed 5,000 four-page *Courier* supplements highlighting amenities of the Polson-Flathead Lake life styles. He urged the Northern Pacific Railway to sell through tickets to Flathead Lake.

He leased space in the Flathead County State Bank and McIntire buildings and retained a room in the Gray Building near the Grandview Hotel. But the bungalow and electric railway plans never panned out.

In 1917 Colonel White donated three lots in Island Villa to the State of Montana for use as bird refuges.

He also invested in other Montana properties. He acquired promising commercial properties in Butte and he sold 235 acres at the west entrance to Glacier Park to U.S. Parks Commissioner Mather who donated the land to the government. The colonel also planned to develop some 435 acres in the Missoula area.

But Flathead Lake was the apple of his eye. In advertisements, Colonel White called the area "a dimple on the cheek of nature."

In 1919 he was reported ill and was treated for blood poisoning for a scraped knee at the "Sisters' Hospital." Colonel White decided to winter in California but before he heft, he held an excursion for new teachers and others – and an auto-boat-train tour to Kalispell and back. The Polson Chamber of Commerce feted the colonel with a banquet a few days later.

Still dreaming of a golden future in 1919, the colonel pledged a seven-month long advertising campaign to the end July 26, 1920, with a six-day auction of eleven miles of villa sites owned by him. He promised that the Great Northern and Northern Pacific would offer reduced rates to people going to the sale via 61-day round trip tickets and special reduced rates for Polson accommodations for those attending the sale. And he said he would charter the steamer Klondike and a large covered barge for a week to carry prospective purchasers to the sites. There would be a band and free lunch on the boat. Sales would be made from a barge, parked alongside the Klondike when it was anchored in front of lots being sold. Those events never took place either.

A 1920 newspaper account reported he had moved his main office from St. Paul, Minnesota, to Butte. Nothing was heard from about Colonel White in 1921, but in 1922 he said he planned to return to the Flathead, that it was "time to start another boom in the Flathead Country." However, he and his wife Marian got to Kalispell un late November. But in 1923 the dream machine was working overtime. In January it was reported that Colonel White had filed for water rights to Bad Rock Powersite on the Middle Fork of the Flathead River. He said he would offer the water rights to Henry Ford if the auto magnate would build a factory in that area

.   In May 1923, the commissioners of newly formed Lake County asked for resale of White's villa sites. In December, final action was promised within 60 days. In 1924 White obtained several extensions of deadlines and did hold a sale in August but with disappointing results. Another sale was held July 7, 1925, also with disappointing results.

So just who was Colonel White? Biographical details of his life vary as to birth date and background, and even the spelling of his first name – Almon or Almond. None of the details disclosed the origin of the title "Colonel."

Perhaps the most authentic background is given in *Montana – Its Story and Biography, Vol. III,* published in 1921 by the American Historical Society under the editorial supervision of Tom Stout.

A biographical sketch stated that he was born June 18, 1841 in Whiting, Addison County, Vermont. He was a descendant of the Peregrines, a family who came to America on the Mayflower. He graduated at the age of 18 from Lawrence University, Appleton, Wisconsin, and on graduation day he enlisted in Company E of the 40th Wisconsin Infantry. In the Civil War, he became a sergeant and served as a picket guard around the approaches to Memphis.

After the war he took up civil engineering and was an accountant and bookkeeper, employed by the Chicago and Northwestern Railroad for four years. Railroad officials sent him to Kansas in 1868 to build rail lines. For four years, he supervised 2,000 men and 500 teams, returning to Chicago with a nest egg of $15,000.

The historical publication credited White with laying out 60 townsites in Minnesota, North Dakota, Montana, Washington and Oregon. It was reported he came to Montana in 1890 "on a mission for James J. Hill, president of the Great Northern Railroad" with instructions to "locate a townsite in the most eligible and scenic point of Flathead Valley." In that capacity he purchased 1,000 acres including the townsite of Kalispell and "organized the Kalispell Townsite Company and served as its vice president and managing director 24 years."

He married Marian L. Knight, whose mother was a descendant of Daniel Webster, in Fort Scott, Kansas. The couple had two children – a son Almond A. Jr., who died at the age of 14, and a daughter, Cecil, who graduated with high honors from Mount Vernon Seminary, Washington, D.C., after having attended Dickey College in Moorhead, Minnesota, for one year, St. Mary's Hall in Faribault, Minnesota, for two years, Mrs. Sylvanias Reed's School in New York City for two years. She was fluent in English, French, Italian, German and Spanish.

Miss Cecil was a world traveler, crossing the ocean 16 times. In 1916, she married the Indian Consul in Spain and in 1921 was residing in Barcelona.

Although Colonel White died in 1930 in Blois, France, the estate was not probated in Montana until February 1943 when a Notice of Creditors was published. Probate was not declared fully discharged until June 18, 1957. The total Lake County estate totaled less than $3,500 and consisted of the following villa site lots: Eleven in Cromwell, two in Grouse, six in Festou, six in White Swan, one in Matterhorn, six in Safety Bay and four in Wild Horse.

No heirs were located for the Montana probate and the property was sold to highest bidders, for a total of $1,736. Various fees – for attorney, public administrators, legal publications, filing and more – amounted to $1,705.93. The balance of $30.07 was paid to the State of Montana.

Bill Barba

Bill Barba was man of many interests — aviator, artist, metal sculptor, inventor, old car/trains/planes enthusiast, model builder, diver, adventurer — and perhaps best of all, a genuinely caring person.

When I first met Bill he had just come to the Flathead Lake area and was camped in a tent below what would become his Silver Rock Pines subdivision near Big Arm.

His most public recognition came from his construction of a replica World War I vintage Austin SE-5A fighter plane. Besides flying it around Flathead and Mission Valley skies, he flew it to air shows in Missoula, Kalispell, Reno, Oregon, Washington and Alberta.

Each trip was an adventure including difficulties with Canadian customs officials and sometimes challenging wind conditions. Once, while flying near Butte he said a strong headwind was actually blowing him backwards. At Reno he allowed nationally known racing plane pilots to fly the SE-5A.

And he was a crowd favorite as he donned his Snoopy helmet and mask as he flew by as if looking for the infamous Red Baron.

Wherever he and his plane went they attracted media attention which brought a lot of favorable publicity to Polson and the Flathead Lake area.

For a while he loaned the plane to the Oregon Air and Space Museum and then went to Eugene, Ore., to disassemble the plane enough to fit on his homemade flatbed trailer and haul it back to his Silver Rock Pines residence.

There he went over with meticulous care to put it back in flying condition, updating it with a larger propeller and realigning the engine, then hauling it to the Polson airport and reassembling it. He eventually sold the plane to a buyer in The Netherlands.

But flying was only one of his interests. He bought an old German electric train set from his sister-in-law in Cottonwood, Calif., and purchased an Andean village railroad diorama from a former Hollywood set builder in Missoula. It was such an extensive layout that he partitioned off a room in his basement to accommodate the set. In addition to locomotives, rail cars and trackage, the set had town buildings, a depot, water tower, gas station, bridges, jungle scenery, an Incan temple, animal and people figures, vehicles and more. One thing was missing, though, a system of roads. So he modified the set to include roads and tunnels.

Barba's sense of humor was evident when he crafted a five-ft. high tin-armored Spanish warrior equipped with a sound system and tape that could greet visitors as they entered through the front door of his Silver Rock Pines home. Kids loved that one! Among other projects were a wood-carved bear in a barrel, an ice boat powered by an engine and propeller, and metal sculpted cowboys.

For years I encouraged Bill to write his life story, but he never seemed to have time to get around to it.

I feel so fortunate to have known Bill Barba. He'll be missed.

The late Bill Barba in his home-built replica WWI SE-5A fighter plane.

Paul Fugleberg photo

Among other things

Some really dumb stories

English ain't easy

It's understandable why many immigrants prefer to continue to speak their native language. English can be downright confusing.

I'll give you a few examples:

The metal lead is pronounced led but the present tense of the verb lead should never be said led.

And how 'bout read? Read can be red and red can be read, but never is red read read unless you mis-read red read instead of read.

Even the simplest words can be defined differently – such as "can." There's can the helping verb; can, the verb to preserve vegetables and fruits; can, the noun as in tin or aluminum and can the colloquial term for bathroom, or can, the slangy term meaning to terminate employment, score a basket, discard something. Then there's can-can, the lively dance.

You could say, "Before I do the can-can, I can can some beans, can the lazy hired hand (laborer not fist), open a can of soup and run to the can."

Among other homonymous words of diverse definition are won and one, which reminds me when playing basketball with the kids I never won one-on-one. Among others are fair and fare; core and corps, piece and peace; pair and pare; peal and peel; fairy and ferry; ail and ale; bail and bale; pail and pale; flare and flair, hail and hale; lean and lien, seen and scene, mail and male; two, to and too -- not to mention tutu; while and wile; which and witch; sight, site and cite; dear and deer; bare and bear; mite and might; rite and right; beer and bier; wind and wind, wood and would, or and ore, turn and tern; board and bored; rumors and roomers

Remember the song *"Rumors Are Flying?"* A person just learning the language hearing that might think that the boarding house just exploded.

And there are the different meanings to the word sweep. Can't you just picture the bride with a broom sweeping up the aisle (not isle) as she approaches the groom (the husband-to-be, not the stable hand) as he waits for her at the altar (not alter)?

Those are just a few. How many more can you think of?

The perils of phonetic spelling

Phonetic spelling of words has its pitfalls, too, as shown below.

The late Maynard Nixon gave me a hand-lettered item from an obscure source that also illustrates how difficult English can be. Whoever composed the piece, really wrote it like it sounded:

Won knight a suite, deer little buoy, the sun of a grate kernel, flu up the rode swift as a dear. He stopped at a gnu house and wrang the belle. His tow hurt hymn and he kneaded wrest. He was two tired too raze his fare pail face. A feint mown of pane rows from his lips.

The made who herd the belle wring was about two pair a pear of pares, but she through them down and ran with awl her mite four fear her guessed wood not weight. Butt when she saw the little won, tiers stood inn her ayes at the site.

"Ewe pore deer, why due yew lye hear? Are ewe dyeing?"

"Know," he said. "Eye am feint two the corps."

She boar hymn inn her arms, as she aught, too a room where he mite bee quiet, gave hymn sum bred and meet, held cent under his knows, tied his choler, rapped hymn warmly, gave hymn sum suite drachm from a viol, till at last he went fourth hail as a young hoarse. His ayes shown and his knows was as read as a flour.

Montana name game

Creating a state name game can give you something different to do while waiting for a blizzard to ease, a vacation rainstorm to let up so you can go fishing, or if you just have too much time on your hands. Let your imagination run wild and you can come up some of the goofiest stories. Like this one I call "Coffee klatch at Coffee Creek," a Montana name game. The names of cities, towns and landmarks are in italics.

In any *Montana City* – from *Absarokee* to *Zurich* – cars are great debate topics. Recently in the *Coffee Creek* Café near *Lewistown, Brady Baker, Chester Lloyd, Kevin Hall, Norris Kinsey, Raymond Myers, Roy Stockett* and some of their cronies sat around the table at their morning coffee break and took every *Opportunity* to argue.

A *Great Falls* attorney, *Tyler Tracy,* started the debate by saying, "I'll bet a month's *Billings* I can tell you the kinds of cars that *Madison* and *Jefferson* would have driven."

"A *Lincoln,* guessed banker *Craig Dooley.* Dependable, secure, they could *Hopp* in and drive from *Saltese* to *Amsterdam* via *Glasgow* and back through *Manhattan* and *Harlem* to the *Potomac."*

"I disagree," snorted owly *Morgan Proctor,* who with his wife *Dagmar,* had recently moved to the area from their *Homestead* near *Ronan.* You've got bats in your *Belfry.* They would've driven a *Frazer."*

"No way, no more than *Lewis and Clark* would have had a Peerless," chimed in *Dean Chance,* a copper miner from *Butte. "*You can bet your *Pony* on it."

"You guys can't *Buffalo* me,*"* interrupted *Warren Roberts,* a farmer in the *Dell* area. "They would've driven a *Franklin."*

"Why?" asked *Elmo Fife,* the *Barber.*

"Because they were solid as a *Silver Gate.* They had the grace of a *Black Eagle* and could glide down the highway, never even *Fishtail* while rounding *Bowman's Corner."*

Just then *Winston Dutton,"* a jet set *Emigrant* from *Judith Gap,"* burst through the door, looking as lean as a *Hungry Horse.*

"Hi, guys. Just flew in from *Tampico.* Oh, no, it *Simms* like you're arguing again. What about this time?"

"Famous people's cars," replied *Rudyard Sheridan Custer,* a bald, retired army *Reserve* general from *Lodge Grass* near *Hardin.*

Winston, who fancied himself quite a wit, asked, "All right, what must a car have if it has no brakes?"

"A *Bighorn,"* the men hooted.

"Ah, your collective *Wisdom* exceeds only that of a *Lame Deer,* a *Whitetail* at that," *Winston* chortled.

A sudden silence ensued, making it *Plains* that it was a poor choice of words. There wasn't even time for *Winston* to *Fallon* on his knees and *Pray* for forgiveness before the fireworks started.

"Two-thirds of a pun is p-u," moaned *Clancy Condon.* You *Otter* get your *Moccasin* outa here. Go sit on a *Geyser,* or soak your head in a wash *Basin,* jump into *Flathead Lake,* climb *Iron Mountain,* and get lost in the *Highwood,"* *Clancy* shouted, working up a good head of steam. "I think I'll *Belt* you one!"

With a face as flushed as a *Redstone, Winston* warned with a *Superior* air, "You *Boyes* better not be mean to me. I'm quite *Poplar* and influential in the *Capitol* in *Helena,* you know."

Surly *Carter Carlyle,* whose temper would *Acton* the least provocation, said with a *Savage* snarl, "You know that *Lonepine,* the only tree in the *Rock Springs* national forest between *Angela* and *Cohagen…*"

As *Carter* rose from his chair, *Mildred Danvers,* the waitress with the *Floweree Rosebud* print apron, took command.

Armed with *Three Forks* with a distinct new *York* accent, she ordered, "OK, you *Boyds,* no *Moore!* I'll *Stanford* no rough stuff here. I'll *Collins Marshal Dillon* if I have to."

Roscoe Hathaway, editor of the *Big Arm* Weekly Muscle, made a peaceful overture. "C'mon, fellows, this is a *Pleasant valley,* a regular *Eden.* No violence now. Let's get back to famous people's cars. This'll make a better story than a *Watson Glen* race."

"I agree," said *Edgar Elliston,* a forest ranger en route from *Missoula* to *Kalispell.* "If you ask me, I'd say *Jackson* would have liked a *Jackson,* of course, but *Cleveland* would have preferred a *Drummond* and *Harrison* an *Essex.* "

"Yeah, and *Grant* would've insisted on a *Jordan.* That was faster than a *Wild Horse* chasing an *Antelope* on the *Grassrange* – especially west of *Laredo,*" asserted *Lindsay Livingston.*

"That was west of *Laramie,* dummy," snorted *Shelby Townsend,* a grizzled old *Shepherd.*

"Whatever," *Terry Thurlow* added quickly, trying to avert another argument. "I think that *Roosevelt* would have had an old *Lambert* if he had been able to find one. He had to drive around *Fort Peck* in *Raynesford.* Incidentally, *Garfield* would have liked an *Austin.* "

"Naw, you're thinking of *Churchill,* " said *Mosby Moorehead,* whose grandfather had been an English remittance man ranching along the *Musselshell* between *Roundup* and *Melstone.* "

The attorney who had initiated the *Ringling* circus-type debate, said, "You could *Yaak* about this all *Somers* long. Who's gonna buy this coffee?"

Victor Sheffield, retired after *Sixteen* years as a professional gambler, said, "I'll bet your *Twin Bridges* to my *Four Buttes* it won't be me."

"Oh, be *Quietus,* " *Tracy* retorted. "This is a *Richland;* someone *Hanover* some of that *Gold Creek Lustre.* "

"I'll pay *Fergus* and me," volunteered *Logan Slayton,* "but the rest of you *Outlook* for yourselves, wish on a *Silver Star* or roll a *Paradise* to see who'll *Winnett.* "

"Worry not, gentlemen," voiced a stranger dressed in white. "Allow me the *Liberty* of picking up the tab. I've enjoyed listening. I had heard of your unusual coffee break conversations. Now I have a *Fairview* of how things are."

"Thank you, sir," *Tracy* acknowledged, peering quizzically at the unusual *Circle* of light around the stranger's head. "Have I seen you *Pryor* to today? Who are you?"

"No, you haven't, but you'll see me again. I'm *St. Peter* – from *Heaven's Peak.* "

Polson's Cherry Pit Spit Splat

In August 1985 "Polson's Cherry Pit Spit Splat" marked the close of a successful cherry harvest.

The rules were tang-tongueling:

Within the Pit Spit Splat Spit Pit, competition pitted top spitters in several pit-spitting classes: Short, middle and long range pit spitting; trick pit spitting and the main event – a spot spit spitting spectacular specifically based on accuracy.

The event pitted top pit spitters of all other pit spit contests against one another in cherry pit spot-spitting. Target was a large cherry pit spot-spit spit pot in which to spot-spit spit pits.

The grand champion cherry pit spit splat pit spitter won a trophy, a 20-pound lug of cherries (unspit) and the spit pit spot-spit spittoon into which the spot-spit pits were spat.

Runners up received ribbons and were offered wheelbarrows in which to haul away the spot-spit pits.

In case of a tie, the winner would be selected by reciting the following in the fastest time with fewest mistakes:

How many cherry pits would Charley, the champion cherry pit spitter spit if Charley could spit pits? Twice as many if he'd split pits to spit and spit split pits. If he didn't split pits to spit and spat unsplit pits, he'd spit only half the pits he'd have spat had he spit the unsplit pits.

Fortunately, there was no tie and no one strangled on a tongueled tang.

Flathead Nessie Interview

(August 2001)

After five years the Flathead Monster has reappeared, according to an article in the *Missoulian*. Fish, Wildlife and Parks Manager Jim Vashro stated the sighting was reported by "a reliable source" on August 18 near Gravel Bay on the East Shore of Flathead Lake.

An angler was reeling in a small lake trout and a "large form – judged to be several feet long – was observed for several seconds tracking the hooked fish as it neared the surface. The object's shape … and tail fin were characteristic of a sturgeon."

It was the first sighting since 1996.

Well, that was great news. I'd been concerned about Montana's Flathead Nessie although he/she/whatever had disappeared for several years at a time before. After all, it's been around since 1889 and you never know what might happen at the age of 109.

Anyway, using a special piscatorial hot line translator we got in touch with Nessie and asked the lake's resident denizen where it has been. The conversation went something like this:

PF: How come no one has seen you since 1996?

N: I got tired of the paparazzi – so many people trying to catch or photograph me. I decided to go on vacation. Had a close call up by Woods Bay in 1993 when those two guys with a video camera almost got a definitive picture of me. Only view I gave them, though, was an inconclusive shadowy blob.

PF: I remember that. So, where did you go?

N: Oh, all over the world. You guys have the Interstate highway network. We monsters have the Subterranean Intercontinental — quite a network. First I swam down to visit my old buddy, the Pend Oreille Paddler, near Sandpoint, Idaho. Then I headed up to see the cousins at Lake Okanagan, British Columbia. Almost had Ogopogo persuaded to swim out to Lake Champlain on the New York-Vermont border and visit our Uncle Champ. But Ogopogo decided the exchange rate was too disadvantageous for Canadian visitors, A "fin" there would only be worth $3.30 – a 34 percent discount. Outrageous!

PF: I understand. I had forgotten that you Nessies sometimes swim in pairs.

N: That and more. Remember that incident on the West Shore in the '50s where a whole bunch of us were sighted?

PF: Yeah, below the Flathead Lookout.

N: That's right. Actually, that was a convention we Nessies were having – and one of the seminars was to record human reactions at sudden sightings of aquatic creatures. Boy, they were chattering like a bunch of monkeys. Carloads of 'em. And nobody had a camera!

PF: Where did you go from Okanagan?

N: Lake Champlain. Stayed there around there for a couple years freeloading on Champ and other relatives, but my allergies caused me to move on.

Leslie Griffith shows the 181-lb sturgeon he claims to have caught in Flathead Lake.
Meiers Studio photo

PF: Allergies?

N: Yeah, something in the water, I guess. In fact, sometimes I think I detect it in Flathead. You guys better watch out what you're letting come into the lake. I'd started sneezing and these big waves would appear out of nowhere. Anyway, from there I went over to Lake Baikal in what I thought was still the Soviet Union.

PF: You didn't know about the breakup? It was in the news.

N: Don't be stupid. You can wrap a fish in newspaper, but that doesn't mean he can read. No, I didn't know. I stayed there until recently, but I heard boaters talking about how bad things were getting. Food was short and I was afraid they might take a liking to Nessies, so I high-finned it outa there. I'd been away from Montana for five years and I was getting kinda homesick. Stopped in Loch Ness to see Grandpa Nessie but he was out cavorting somewhere. He's pretty frisky for someone his age.

PF: When did you get back?

N: In early July. But I was almost wishing I hadn't come back. Darned near got killed.

PF: What happened?

N: Well, I was floating along just beneath the surface, minding my own business when suddenly the KwaTaaNuk Princess came along and gave my whiskers a buzz cut. That startled me so bad I had a fin-jerk reaction and bumped the bottom of the boat. Caused it to leak enough so they had to get the Polson Fire Department boat to help 'em pump water out so they could get back to port. Sorry 'bout that. It was unintentional.

PF: Did you find that things had changed much around Flathead?

N: Nope. You're still debating issues like a four-lane vs. super two Highway 93, gambling, sales tax and state-tribal fishing and bird hunting permits. Forest fires are keeping me in deep water right now. I'm allergic to smoke, you know. I feel a sneeze coming on and I don't want to cause a seiche that would inundate Polson and maybe wipe out Kerr Dam.

PF: Okay, I guess you'd better go. Good to hear that you're back. Be seein' ya.

N: I hope not.

Multi-tasking woes

I have trouble with multitasking. Researching for this book was a real exercise in multi-tasking. As I delved into the many things that I had written over the past 57 years, it was easy to get sidetracked.

The best part of research reveals joy at the accomplishments of people I've written about and of the pleasures of writing about and photographing interesting places that I visited.

Occasional coffee klatch comments can lead to nonsensical, goofy, off-the wall pieces. That happened following a coffee break discussion of the successful cloning of sheep and cattle. Some scientists began talking about the possibility of cloning body parts.

I pondered the wisdom of the trend. F'rinstance, suppose there were a couple clever cloners called Clyde and Clutie. That could cause considerable consternation if they got goo-goo eyed over each other, married and created a clan of their clones.

Endowed with common characteristics, each would have the human traits of free will, the ability to choose right from wrong – and some would opt for wrong as they grew. It happens in the best of families even now, you know.

A couple cracked clones from Clyde and Clutie's clan could cause chaotic confusion. Can you imagine the headlines following a crime spree?

Cracked clones cast into clink; cops claim cracked clone Clancy committed crimes. Or, *cute Clutie's careless clonette, Cathy, caught conducting con scam.*

So the case goes to court. So far, so good? Not really. More headlines: *Crafty counselor claims incorrect clone canned; Clumsy clone Clifford committed crime, not Clancy. Or, Cathy clonette cites coercion, cancels scam confession.*

After reviewing the facts, the judge dismisses the case citing insufficient, inconclusive evidence; all characteristics are identical – fingerprints, DNA, eye and hair color, etc.

Enter the ACLU championing a new cause – cloned rights, and correctly so. More headlines: *Advocates charge Clancy clone illegally cast into calaboose; classy Cassie, clone clan's beauty queen, charged with con scam; cute Clutie clonette cleared.*

Can't be too cautious with cloning. It can create imperfect perfection.

The traditional way to create families is preferable. Besides, there's a lot more joy in the old-fashioned way!

Thoughtversation

For years there have been radio telescopes and other scientific devices listening and transmitting various sounds or impulses to outer space in attempts to determine whether or not there are forms of intelligent life in the universe. In late June 1989, there was even a concentrated effort to have folks join in an experiment of mass transmission of thought waves.

Just for kicks, I took part in the exercise. Don't know if anyone else made contact, but I did – sort of. It was an interesting thoughtversation. It went like this:

"Hey, is anybody out there?"

Silence.

"Anybody listening? Is anybody out there?"

Still silence.

"For the third time, is anybody out there?"

Then came a mysterious reply: "Yup."

"Where are you?"

"Ain't gonna tell."

"Why not?"

"Because you might find me."

"Well, I should hope we would. Why don't you want us to find you?"

"I'll tell you why. I've been observing you for many years. You have nothing to offer me, only trouble."

"What do you mean?"

"My observations disclose a human nature prone to wars, threats of wars, disease, greed, intolerance, racial and religious discrimination, and sins of commission and omission."

"True enough, but we're working hard trying to turn things around. We were kinda hopin' you'd have some advice to give us."

"I'll tell you this much: Look within as well as beyond."

"What do you mean by that?"

"Nothing that you don't know already in your mind and heart."

"If you won't tell me where you are, at least tell me your name."

"Well, I'm not as far away as you think – and my initials are PHF."

"PHF?"

"Yup."

"Gee, that's funny. Those are my initials."

"Not funny at all. This is your conscience speaking."

Uff da stories

Uff da. That's the closest description I can give to explain the impact of the latest viral onslaught that has been attacking so many local residents recently.

Like the persistent California rainstorms of this winter, this Uff da bug is relentless and unyielding as it marches inexorably through the various anatomical passages of the human frame – leading to an aching head to running noses, then stuffed up nasal passages, down a throat so sore that swallowing is an ordeal, into the chest cavities where congestion produces wheezing, shortness of breath, rib wracking coughing jags, resulting in over-all tiredness and lethargy.

Did I leave out anything? Possibly the compound astigmatism of the ear drums! You could count on your two hands the times over a 50-year period that I've missed work for reasons other than emergencies or surgery. But the Uff da bug laid me low from Saturday through Wednesday. There's a bright side to the situation though. I've lost 10 pounds. But there are easier ways to lose weight and I can be naturally lazy without all the side effects.

So what's with Uff da? It's an expression inherited from my Norwegian grandmother, who would Uff da her way through the various vicissitudes of everyday life.

Two incidents come to mind nearly 70 years later:

"Uff da," Grandma said while reading the newspaper, "the price of mutton is only five cents a pound at the Grand Central Market." A few minutes later Grandma took me in tow and we rode the streetcar all the way from the San Fernando Valley to downtown Los Angeles. The streetcar ride was much more enjoyable than having to eat that nickel-a-pound mutton.

Grandma's frugality was unlimited. One day while visiting her home, I made brief pit stop and flushed the toilet. As I came out of the bathroom, Grandma met me at the door waving her finger, "Uff da, Paul, you only need to flush after you've done a big yob."

I checked the10-inch thick dictionary in the newspaper office to see if Uff da was defined by the lexicographers. It wasn't. But on the fridge at home is a magnetic sign that gives some definitions of the popular Scandahoovian expression. Among them are:

"Uff da is looking in the mirror and discovering you're not getting better, you're just getting older."

"Uff da is trying to dance the polka to rock and roll music."

"Uff da is arriving late for a lutefisk supper and getting served minced ham instead."

"Uff da is looking in the rear view mirror and seeing flashing red lights."

"Uff da is noticing non-Norwegians at a church dinner using lefse as napkins."

Well, those are just a few examples. There's many more. Yah sure, you betcha.

Ah, procrastination

Many folks make New Year's resolutions. Me, too. I usually resolve to renew my procrastination tendencies – when I get around to it.

The procrastinator's guideline of "Never do anything today that can be put off until tomorrow" pays off more often than you might think.

F'instance, I put off trading in my red '67 Ford Galaxie for so long that the trade-in was worth considerably more than what I paid for the car in the first place.

Saved a bundle of money, too, when our household of seven persons got by with one bathroom. We talked about adding a second bathroom for years, but never got around to it.

Procrastination could play beneficial roles worldwide. Wars could be delayed or canceled, riots and revolutions avoided, tax hikes deferred, unqualified political candidates might not make up their minds soon enough to run for office – some, however, don't procrastinate when they really should.

You might think that procrastination is a strange trait for anyone engaged in newspaper work with its deadlines.

Well, not necessarily. Sometimes by waiting until the last minute to do a story, we would end up with late breaking developments. Some would call that rationalization. I called it strategy – when it worked. When it didn't … never mind.

Another thing: The more you put off doing something, the more time you have to do some of the other things that you've put off.

Admitted, some of these things can be so enjoyable that you secretly wonder why you deferred them. Fishing, a train trip, Alaskan cruise, stuff like that.

To write properly about the additional benefits of procrastination requires taking a note book, sitting in the shade of a tall tree along the lake shore and doing some serious philosophizin'.

By golly, I think I'll do just that – when I get around to it.

Just for the pun of it

Puns are fun. They're not limited to any subject, nor are they limited by national or international borders. Here are some, some old some new:

The Tibetan housewife, smelling something burning, rushed into her kitchen and exclaimed, "Oh, my baking yak!"

Egyptian back-straighteners are called Cairo-practors.

Off Taiwan the other day a ship with a cargo of yo-yos sank -- 184 times.

On the farm:

You can harness a chicken to a grain bin, but it can't pullet.

Propaganda is a socially proper goose.

An irate farmer stopped a neighbor taking a couple sheep across a frozen pond: "You can't take your sheep that way -- nobody can pull the wool over my ice."

Musical puns:

A fish with perfect pitch is known as a piano tuna.

The irritable music critic wrote "The song was written in C, sung in D, and sounded like H."

Then there's the razor blade theme song, "Nobody knows the stubble I've seen."

Micscllaneous

Recently there was a report from California that a couple freighters collided, resulting in a large spill of red paint. No injuries, but the crews were marooned.

The world is a puzzle with a peace missing.

A legislative committee is a group that keeps minutes but wastes hours.

Inflation is a stab in the buck.

A Scottish anthropologist digging deep found copper wire estimated to be 100 years old. He figured that the Scots had an elaborate lighting system a century ago. Then a British excavator dug twice as deep and found copper wire estimated to be 200 years old – a sign that the Brits had an elaborate communication system way back when. But up in Minnesota Ole and Sven dug an even deeper hole – and found absolutely nothing. Ole said, "Sven, I tink our ancestors discovered wireless communication."

Autobiography: Your car's life story.

Stucco: What you get when you sit on gummo.

Hythtory ith a mythtery

My friends George and Helen Thomas in Seattle sent me these historical definitions purportedly coming from sixth grade history tests. Maybe they were and maybe they weren't sixth graders – seems I'd heard some of them before, but you might get a chuckle from them:

Ancient Egypt was inhabited by mummies and they all wrote in hydraulics. They lived in the Sarah Dessert. The climate of the Sarah is such that all the inhabitants have to live elsewhere.

The Greeks were a highly sculptured people, and without them we wouldn't have history. The Greeks also had myths. A myth is a female moth.

Moses led the Hebrew slaves to the Red Sea where they made unleavened bread, which is bread made without any ingredients. Moses went up on Mount Cyanide to get the ten commandments. He died before he ever reached Canada.

Solomon had three hundred wives and seven hundred porcupines.

Socrates was a famous Greek teacher who went around giving people advice. They killed him. Socrates died from an overdose of wedlock. After his death, his career suffered a dramatic decline.

In the Olympic games, Greeks ran races, jumped, hurled biscuits, and threw the java.

Julius Caesar extinguished himself on the battlefields of Gaul. The Ides of March murdered him because they thought he was going to be made king. Dying, he gasped out: "Tee hee, Brutus."

Joan of Arc was burnt to a steak and was canonized by Bernard Shaw.

Gutenberg invented removable type and the Bible. Another important invention was the circulation of blood. Sir Walter Raleigh is a historical figure because he invented cigarettes and started smoking.

Sir Francis Drake circumsized the world with a 100-foot clipper.

The greatest writer of the Renaissance was William Shakespeare. He was born in the year 1564, supposedly on his birthday. He never made much money and is famous only because of his plays. He wrote tragedies, comedies, and hysterectomies, all in Islamic pentameter.

Writing at the same time as Shakespeare was Miguel Cervantes. He wrote Donkey Hote. The next great author was John Milton. Milton wrote Paradise Lost. Then his wife died and he wrote Paradise Regained.

Beethoven wrote music even though he was deaf. He was so deaf he wrote loud music. He took long walks in the forest even when everyone was calling for him. Beethoven expired in 1827 and later died for this.

Delegates from the original 13 states formed the Contented Congress. Thomas Jefferson, a Virgin, and Benjamin Franklin were two singers of the Declaration of Independence. Franklin discovered electricity by rubbing two cats backward and declared, "A horse divided against itself cannot stand." Franklin died in 1790 and is still dead.

Special people

Mary Lou

As countless other couples have learned, nearly 40 years – or any prolonged time together – a bond is forged by love and shared experiences of joy and sorrow, good times and hardship, health and sickness, frustration and forgiveness.

When death snaps that bond, it's devastating. Such is the price of love. But it's worth it, and I'd do it all over again if I could, albeit with the benefits of hindsight and maturity to soften the rough spots and enhance the good ones.

These were a few of the thoughts that swept over me like and avalanche during the weeks preceding my wife's death on Feb. 11, 1996.

I'd like to tell you about all her attributes, but there isn't space – and she wouldn't want me to. Suffice it to say that through her caring, kind, generous spirit, she touched more lives than she ever knew. Her courage and determination displayed in fighting a combined set of debilitating illnesses were admired and appreciated.

How or why I was so lucky to have met her among all the people on earth, and for her to become my wife, I'll never know. But I'm glad it worked out that way, and I thank God for Mary Lou.

Our son Mark in 1986 wrote this song for his mother. It really reflects the depth of love she had for her family:

Tears of Love

Hey, do you remember when
we were living at home?
When everyday was made for fun
And playing out all day long?

We'd sit in the swing, fly high and sing to the clouds
and momma would stand in the kitchen looking out.
I used to wonder what she was feeling but then I'd see her smile,
And I could tell those were tears of love in her eyes.

Hey, do you remember when
we were living at home?
When Saturdays were made for fun
and playing out all day long?

We'd head to the back with our baseball bats – dad would pitch the ball
and momma would stand in the window watching it all.
I used to wonder to wonder if she was sad but then I'd see her smile,
And I could tell that those were tears of love in her eyes

Then one day the moment came we'd waited for all our lives.
We packed our bags and moved to the city lights.
To us it took forever. But to momma it was overnight.
I remember saying goodbye. And all the tears that momma cried.

Every now and then I remember when we were living at home,
When every day was made for fun
and playing out all day long.

When memories get too much for me I give her a call
to tell her everything that's going on.
And sometimes when we hang up, I hear momma cry.
But I know those are tears of love in her eyes.

Momma's still got those tears of love in her eyes.
Those are tears of love in momma's eyes.

Jimmy

Our son, Jimmy, wasn't very big – only about 19 ½ inches in length and six and a half pounds, four ounces in weight when he was born Oct. 15, 1965. He was never noticed in the myriad of headlines reporting fast-breaking news in this fast-moving world. The drama in which he figured has been experienced by many parents time and again around the world – and, unfortunately, will be repeated in the future. As such, the incident went down in official record books as a set of birth and death statistics.

Despite his lack of physical stature and his extremely brief life span – about 48 hours – Jimmy is going to be remembered by this writer and his family as long as they live.

He carried a mighty big impact. In his 48 hours of life on this planet, Jimmy brought our family a heap of living – all the emotions that can ever be encountered in anyone's lifetime, anywhere, anyplace, anytime.

He was quite a fellow.

Doc Eggensperger

Kermit A. (Doc) Eggensperger, longtime editor and publisher of the Sanders County Ledger, died in January 1997 in Fort Smith, Arkansas. Doc was one of the most respected and effective weekly newsmen in Montana.

Although he retired as publisher in 1983, he continued to write his weekly column and did some reporting. He was diagnosed with a benign cranial brain tumor in 1993. Surgery resulted in disrupted sense of balance and affected his speech. Despite the difficulties, his determination and spirit was sustained. Through his wife, Maxine, he continued his convey his thoughts and memories in the column;

Doc promoted countless community causes through his editorials and personal efforts. He was the recipient of the Montana Newspaper Association's highest award, Master Editor/Publisher. In addition, he served on the University of Montana's first Council of 50, was a guest lecturer at the UM journalism school, served on the school board, was active in church work and occasionally delivered the sermon in the Community Congregational Church in Thompson Falls.

He had a delightful and sometimes quirky sense of humor. Our long friendship began shortly after I arrived in Polson in 1959. When he suggested that Noxon Rapids Reservoir boosters kidnap the Flathead Lake monster, I admonished him that the vigilantes had hanged men for less than that. The next week, Press Association secretary Dorothy Johnson wrote both of us, "Sic 'em," that a "feud" would be great for readership.

So feud we did – for years, making journalism perfectionists cringe. Column battles centered on fishing, weather, causes of earthquakes and wind storms, sports, and more. Doc's photograph of bananas being picked from a pine tree in Thompson Falls was exposed as a phony when the *Flathead Courier* proved with pictures that pineapples – not bananas – were picked from pine trees at the Polson golf course.

Our fishing feud resulted in a contest with the Flathead team headed by ex-Governor J. Hugo Aronson. The contest was judged by a biased bunch in Hot Springs who declared Hot Springs the winner by displaying a live pike from Lonepine Reservoir and a large ocean-going skate that came from Seattle's Pike Place fish market. Incidentally, Flathead Lake's entry was a frozen bull trout retrieved from a Bigfork locker while the Noxonites produced a minnow-sized perch. Both sides admitted that fishing was terrible that day.

The only time I couldn't fire back at one of Doc's comments occurred during President Nixon's brief campaign stop at the Glacier Park International Airport at Kalispell during the president's bid for reelection. I was on the press trailer flanked on both sides by photographers with their telephoto lenses, tripods and TV cameras.

The following week in the Sanders County Ledger, Doc ran a picture of me on the trailer and pointed out "The guy with the toy camera is Fugleberg." That "toy camera" was my $99, 35-mm point and shoot outfit. Yet the picture I took remains one of my favorite photos.

Ridiculous? Certainly. Fun? Absolutely. And the readers – some of 'em anyway – seemed to enjoy it. Long-time *Ledger* and *Courier* readers still comment on the feud decades later! We probably wouldn't be able to get away with such shenanigans in today's era of pseudo-sophistication and political correctness.

There was only one Doc Eggensperger. His love of family and community and his sense of humor live on. Thanks, Doc, for some great and enjoyable newspaper years.

From my vantage point on the press trailer during the campaign visit of President Nixon to Kalispell, I used what Doc Eggensperger called a "toy camera" to snap this picture.

The Rose and the petals

Carolyn Heinz

Carolyn Heinz in June 2003 closed her full-time teaching career – after 37 years in the game, 32 of those teaching in Polson. Her versatility is reflected by the various positions held. In Polson she taught grades 1, 2, 4, remedial reading and math in grades 1-8, and 15 years as Gifted and Talented Lab teacher in Linderman, Cherry Valley and Polson Middle School. From 1994 she taught fourth grade at Linderman.

A teacher has awesome challenges and responsibilities. The range of technology, social trends, attitude changes, teaching methods, and ever-changing curriculum require a special type of person to keep up with the changes and yet stay on top of the teaching profession. Carolyn Heinz did just that

Twice she was nominated for the prestigious national Maryfrances Shreeve Award for Teaching Excellence. Endorsements of the nominations made by past and present colleagues and administrators, parents and students show the esteem with which Mrs. Heinz is held.

Here are a few of the remarks:

"Her resourcefulness and willingness to go 'above and beyond the call of duty' to provide an all-encompassing learning environment sets her apart."

"Mrs. Heinz considers the whole child and the various 'intelligences' inherent in different children. She taught that traditional knowledge was not the only measure of intelligence, but that strengths in perceptual areas, music, physical skills and language were valuable as well."

"Her lessons plans are creative, well-planned, interesting, and fun for the children. She demands a lot from her students and consequently the children respond with extra effort."

"I remember her most for her kindness and patience … She gives all students a chance."

"She is committed to teaching each student individually to serve their best interests."

"I now remember how impressed I was with the way she disciplined, so firm and yet so gentle. The children understood what was expected of them and respected her authority."

"Mrs. Heinz makes herself available to the parents to address any concerns they may have."

Some of the creative teaching techniques:

As part of the fourth grade lesson in story writing, she had the children read their stories "aloud to themselves." This was done through a PVC pipe "phone' – made by linking plastic plumbing pipe elbows and bends. When the student holds one end up to his/her ear and whispers into the other end, he can listen to his own voice and can decide whether or not the story flows logically.

When studying medieval ages students donned costumes of the times and learned the roles of kings, knights, pages, serfs, prepared – and ate – foods of that era, developed a market place and entertainment.

"Petals around the Rose" is an observation game that Mrs. Heinz used with fourth grade G/T students to detect hidden patterns in things. A pair of dice was rolled on the table. A rose would be the dot centered on the top of each odd numbered die. A five would be one rose, surrounded by four petals; a three, one rose and two petals; even numbered dice, of course, were all petals.

A former student, now a multimedia producer, wrote "At the time I probably didn't fully understand this lesson, but it wasn't the last time we were taught to look for the hidden potentials … I have discovered the 'petals around the rose' many times since that first exercise. The patterns of life are not always easy to discern, certainly not obvious; but I've learned to look for them – to always anticipate them." Her father was a Methodist minister and her mom a schoolteacher. This automatically meant Carolyn would face frequent moves as she was growing up and would be exposed to different cultures and conditions.

In 1961 her mother, the late Patricia Chalk, launched her daughter on a teaching career when she wrote a poem for her: "There is no greater thing I know, than helping children as they grow … No other task beneath the sun is quite so thrilling as this one."

Each September Carolyn would post the poem above her desk. She said, "That poem and a quote from Aletha Jane Lindstrom's *A Legacy of Rainbows* reflect the foundation of my teaching philosophy. Lindstrom's message was: 'The best learning comes when imaginations roam … Respect each child's enthusiasm. Share your own sense of wonder. Make time for 'hunting rainbows' (even our bad days have bright spots). Help kids find out for themselves."

Two encouraging trends, she sees, are assessments geared to an individual child's growth and recognition of the need to teach "life choices."

An avid gardener, Mrs. Heinz says, "The students I teach remind me of the flowers in my garden. Each is unique, having its own form of beauty. Each grows and matures in its own way, requiring a variety of forms of care."

"Structure" is needed in the classroom to provide students with the feeling of optimism, willingness to reach out, take reasonable risks, learn new concepts and share their ideas.

She defines the strongest forms of structure:

"Love – knowing you are cared for at home and at school.

"Expectations – making reachable goals, moving forward by making small steps, which lead to success with just enough challenge.

"Standards – knowing the boundaries, what is acceptable and what is not, and the logical consequences."

Carolyn continues to be active in the community – in her church and the Caring Community program, and not surprisingly, in school activities including curriculum development, creative arts and as a field trip chaperone. Some writing is also on her to do list.

It's easy to visualize Carolyn Heinz as a rose. All those petals surrounding the rose are the countless children whose lives she has touched.

Blanche Harding, Montana's 'Puppet Lady'

Anyone who knew Blanche Harding, even if only for a few years, has a lifetime of memories – so many that it's hard to decide which are the most memorable. She was so talented. I've whittled down my list to these:

In my mind I still see her driving her station wagon with the license plate reading "Puppets" – heading out of town to do a series of puppet shows for children in schools throughout Montana. She said that she had the most interesting traveling companions. Of course, they were marionettes representing a virtual who's who in Montana history: Artist Charlie Russell, mountain man Jim Bridger, Chief Joseph, railroad empire builder Jim Hill, Copper King Marcus Daly, pioneer rancher Granville Stuart, vigilante X. Beidler, explorers Lewis and Clark and members of their Corps of Discovery, and Sacagawea.

And there were the "ordinary" folks from yesteryear: fun loving cowboy Buffalo Joe and his friends, the Dalton sisters, a couple Virginia City dance hall dollies; and Mrs. Knudson, a Norwegian honyocker's wife.

Sometimes she carried a circus troupe: acrobats Alfredo and Flossy, Tony the juggler; the singing couple, Cowboy Silas and Amanda; Clancey the trapeze artist; Miss Poochie, a poodle that could jump through hoops; Chee Chee the acrobatic monkey, and others.

Another favorite memory is a hand-lettered sign on the side of a box in her workshop. It read, "The abilities you are born with are God's gift to you. What you do with them is your gift to God." It was more than a sign – it was a way for life for Blanche as she shared her talents as puppeteer, artist, teacher, lecturer, and craftsperson to bring enjoyment, entertainment, education and inspiration to countless folks of all ages.

One final memory: Blanche was an encourager – for family, friends, entire communities. Even up to her very last day. I'm so grateful that I had a chance to visit her two weeks before she died. She was typical Blanche, looking ahead, adapting to ever changing conditions, accentuating the positive and eliminating the negative, asking about others, and offering encouragement, encouragement and more encouragement.

What a remarkable lady Blanche Harding was – and what wonderful memories she left with us.

Carmine Mowbray

Carmine Mowbray and husband Todd purchased the Flathead Courier and Ronan Pioneer in 1983. Under their ownership our family had the opportunity to continue to keep active in the local newspaper operation. They called me back to fill editorial capacities during vacations, illnesses and in interim situations. My wife Mary Lou was able to continue typesetting up to her final illness, and son Alan worked as photographer and darkroom tech until expanding his own photography business.

The Mowbrays also implemented the merger of the *Courier* and *Pioneer* to form the *Lake County Leader* in 1988 – a move that Lorin Jacobson and I had visualized in the early 1970s but were unable to accomplish. After their divorce Carmine continued to run the paper until selling to Lee Enterprises in 2000

She continues to be active in community activities, went back to college, did substitute teaching, and developed her artistic talents. Carmine paints the big scenic backgrounds for the Port Polson Players productions as well. Among her other interests are flying, motorcycling and she's even played the accordion in community plays. She also produces a Saturday morning program for the Home Ground Radio show on Missoula's PBS station.

I appreciate her kindness to our family and her encouragement to me. I'm especially grateful to Carmine and to Karen and Neal Lewing for organizing the retirement party for me following my heart attack.

Neal and Karen Lewing

Neal and Karen Lewing provide a lot more to the community and to Montana than simply presenting summer theatre with their Port Polson Players productions.

Originally founded by the late Larry and Pat Barsness of Virginia City Players fame, who were lured to Polson by the late John Dowdall, president of First Citizens Bank, the Port Polson Players started as a summer theatre operation as the 5th Ave. Playhouse in 1976 in the old Lincoln School. Neal and Karen Lewing purchased the business in 1979.

After the Lincoln School was razed, the Lewings staged plays in various venues including the Ancient Mariner Dinner Theatre, Polson high school, the Elks Club and the Wolf Den Alley Theatre. In 1986, the Players planned to present summer theatre in a large tent. However, a few days before opening night, a strong windstorm swept through the area and destroyed the tent.

It was a blessing disguise, though, because it led the Players to the present location, the former clubhouse on the "old nine" of the Polson Country Club golf course.

The Lewings have expanded their community outreach by directing community theatre productions during the Christmas season and in the spring. They also direct the high school plays in the fall and spring.

Working with the Mission Valley Foundation for the Arts, the Port Polson Players have renovated the WPA-funded log building and renamed it the John Dowdall Theatre. There they present summer theatre, and at least four other community productions during the year as well as sponsoring a children's drama camp each summer and special concerts.

For several years the Lewings also produced summer plays as the Old Prison Players in Deer Lodge in the old Territorial prison. In 2006, after fire had gutted the landmark Rialto Theatre in Deer Lodge, the Port Polson Players gave a benefit performance to raise funds to help restore the facility.

Their generosity is also appreciated by local area residents as they present skits and songs for local service club activities and community festival events. They even presented a "command performance," of one play in the living room of a terminally ill cancer patient.

Dick and Keenie Christopher

Dick and Keenie Christopher are folks whose lives have effectively influenced and touched countless lives in the community. They've certainly encouraged me over the years.

Dick came to Polson as a pharmacist for Hubbard's Pharmacy. When he eventually purchased the business from Cal Hubbard, he renamed it Harbour Pharmacy to reflect the nautical theme that the business community was developing. During his years in Polson he has been involved in community life including serving several years on the school board. He continues to be active in the Presbyterian Church where he has been an Elder and committee chairman and church school leader. In retirement he's added Presbytery responsibilities to his local church work.

Keenie's work within the Polson Presbyterian Church involved outreach programs that affected many local people. She served as an Elder, Deacon, and committee member, and church school leader over the years, was a charter member of the Copeland Memorial Handbell Ringers and the Presbyterian chancel choir. She also sang with the Mission Valley Chorale. It was a joy participating with her in 1985 in Polson's diamond jubilee play, *Valley Full of Diamond*s. She sponsored Dick and me in a 1985 Cursillo at Camp Marshall, a spiritually rewarding experience.

Despite several years of cancer treatments including surgery, chemo and radiation, she continued her singing and bell ringing until the summer of 2008. Her courage, determination and persistence that prevailed throughout her battle with cancer were inspirational to me and all who knew her. Cancer claimed her life but not her spirit.

Carol Sherick

What can be said after all the other complimentary and appreciative words and thoughts have already been offered? That's my dilemma in attempting to add my personal tribute to Carol Sherick's life.

Among things for which I am grateful are:

1. That Carol lived long enough to learn of the dedication of the Carol Sampson Sherick Memorial Trail, and of the hundreds of folks who attended that dedication honoring her.

2. The overwhelming attendance at her memorial service. The standing room only group of people at Immaculate Conception Church certainly was affirmation of the love, respect and appreciation of the entire community for the type of person Carol was.

3. Carol's note of appreciation that she had asked Emily River to read at the close of the memorial service. The note conveyed Carol's appreciation for her hometown and its residents. Work of all professions, organizations, occupations and services were gratefully acknowledged.

Three incidents I fondly recall involving Carol were:

1. A few years ago I snapped a picture of her at the Polson Fly-in as she was getting into the plane that would take her to 10,000 feet for a tandem parachute jump. After her chute opened, you could hear her joyfully screaming all the way to ground.

2. She appreciated so much the opportunities that high school girls have now in sports activities. That wasn't the case when she was in high school. She commented wistfully, "If we'd had those sports, I would have been soooo good..." I bet she would have too. But she was "soooo good" at building great relationships with people of all ages and positive influences that will last for generations.

3. After Keenie Christopher's recent memorial service, I told Carol that I was sorry to learn that she was facing serious health problems. Yet with that sunshine of a smile, she replied, "Well, everybody has to die sometime. This is just my turn."

Such were the lessons of life – love, respect, responsibility, appreciation and dignity – that were reflected by Carol Sherick's life.

Dr. Tom O'Halloran

Dr. Thomas A. (Tom) O'Halloran, who died Tuesday, Nov. 11, 2008, at the age of 91, was a very special person, appreciated by countless numbers of people he treated during his long medical career. He came to Polson in the mid-1960s and was the family doctor to hundreds of folks here until his retirement in 1996. He delivered many babies, too, including two of ours.

Prior to coming to Polson he practiced medicine in England, Canada and Plains. He also served a tour of duty as a surgeon in the Royal Navy.

A man of varied interests, the Irish-born doctor also imported and trained Connemara ponies and trained hunting dogs. He had a natural gift for story telling and writing. Since his retirement he compiled and printed with the help of his son, Mike, two books of short collections of Irish stories under the title of *The Seanachie Speaks*. He had just completed Volume 2 and felt he had enough material for four more volumes.

As I read them, it was easy to imagine Dr. O'Halloran sitting there telling the stories – with a mischievous glint in his eyes. He added his own particular twist to the stories, bringing them up to date and occasionally changing geographical locations, some to Montana. They are delightful reading with elements of the stuff of life -- humor, sadness, joys and sorrows, philosophical observations, successes and disappointments, and surprising endings.

I hope Mike will print the remaining stories and make the books available for sale. Tom O'Halloran's friends and former patients would love to have them.

I'm so grateful to have known Dr. O'Halloran. May his wife Madeleine and their family always cherish the memories of his special gifts of love, compassion, gentleness, sense of humor and the ability to tell those wonderful Irish stories and fairy tales.

Mel Ruder

Montana lost a true giant of journalism when Mel Ruder, founder, editor and publisher of the Hungry Horse News at Columbia Falls, died at the Soldier's Home in that city. He was Montana's first, and as far as I can remember, the state's only, Pulitzer Prize winner. He earned it for his outstanding coverage of the historic 1964 flood.

His pictures and objective, detailed reporting between 1946 and 1978 when he retired were unsurpassed – anywhere. The Hungry Horse News was a consistent winner in state and national better newspaper competitions. His Bystander personal column was informative, entertaining, sometimes wryly humorous, and homespun. His editorials were succinct, direct and effective.

I first met Mel in 1955 at the annual Montana State Newspaper convention in Miles City. What I remember most was his enthusiasm. Mel was cornering every editor and publisher there and praising the Smith-Corona electric typewriter as a major breakthrough in typing up stories to be sent to the Linotype operators for typesetting! Since then many generations of typesetting improvements evolved and Mel kept up with all of them.

He was generous in his encouragement of young reporters and editors. He sent me notes of encouragement during my time in Roundup and Canton, South Dakota. During my 21 years in Polson, Mel continued the practice as he'd drop a note in the mail complimenting the Flathead Courier on its coverage of a story, a column or a photo. Those notes from someone of Mel's stature were appreciated more than words can say.

When he sold the Hungry Horse News, we feared that no one would ever come close to matching Mel's record. But young Brian Kennedy did come close – quite close – and continued to put out a top quality weekly newspaper. Yet Mel still was tops in my eyes. A few years ago, a book of Mel Ruder photos and comments was published. I wish the book, *Pictures, a Park and a Pulitzer,* had been printed 20 years earlier.

The newspaperman's "30" emblem signifying the end of a story didn't apply to his death. Memories are his work, community involvement, personal example and spirit are ongoing in Montana journalism circles.

Personal reflections

The empty nest

Ecclesiastes 3:1 – *For everything there is a season, and a time for every matter under heaven.*

The beginning of the fall quarter of college always brings flashbacks for many parents.

The drive home from the University of Montana in Missoula had been a quiet, reflective one. The couple had helped their youngest son move clothing, school supplies, posters and miscellaneous materials into the dorm room he would occupy during his freshman year.

Farewells were a mixture of joy, apprehension, love and pain – the same emotions encountered when they sent off their other youngsters to college. But this time was different. From day one they'd recognized that the so-called empty nest was as unavoidable as death. But with 30 years of having kids grow up in the house, that day always seemed far off. Abruptly, the future was now. It struck like an avalanche as they arrived home.

Suddenly there were no emergency laundry jobs, no rush meals to prepare at odd hours, no dental and hair-cut appointments to arrange, no refrigerator shelves to keep full for insatiable appetites, no school clothes to mend, and so on.

Tennis rackets and baseball mitts hung on the wall next to the basement stairs. There were bats, baseballs, softballs, tennis balls and long outgrown small mitts in a basket between the workbench and water heater. In the backyard on the grounds near the backboard and hoop were a couple of basketballs; the window wells contained battered Whiffle baseballs and a well-worn Nerf football. Inside, on the closet shelf were idle games -- Backgammon, Trivial Pursuit, Uno, Pictionary, Monopoly, Scrabble and others.

The house was different – empty bedrooms, eerily neat; a crumbless kitchen counter, lacking tell-tale signs of after-school, mid-evening and late night refrigerator raids; a strangely silent telephone; no kicked-off shoes in the living room; no loud boom boxes either. There was even enough hot water for a lengthy shower.

To put it bluntly, the atmosphere in this strange house was downright weird. The couple wasn't certain they even liked the house any more. For sure, they didn't like the deafening silence. And they both had misgivings about mistakes that parents make over the years – not listening closely, making sometimes unfair judgments, unreasonable reactions and uttering unkind words, and more. It was frustrating.

So, they did what millions of parents have done in similar circumstances for countless generations: They sat down and cried. Lord, how they bawled. Then, when they were as limp as a couple wrung-out dishrags, a strange thing happened.

A sense of peace, comfort, and gratefulness enveloped them like a blanket. They sensed a new appreciation of each child and his and her uniqueness, talents, health and love; and the parents gained a stronger appreciation for one another and for the 30 busy, sometimes hectic years that they had shared and experienced as the kids grew.

Now, a few years later, the kids have sprouted wings like eagles to soar on their own. With added maturity both the children and parents have gained new insights into God's grace and God's plan. They continue to discover how flexible and resilient a human can be with God's help.

Perhaps best of all, the children have forgiven their parents for their shortcoming and vice versa. It stands to reason that if God has forgiven each individual his and her mistakes, then with that same grace, the individual can forgive himself or herself for their own shortcomings.

The nest may be empty, but the hearts of those remaining there are full of love for each of those children and for each other.

Each day is a new day

Just when we've become accustomed to writing 2208 on checks, invoices, letters, etc., here it is Jan. 1, 2009, and time to shift gears again. All of which brings to mind that each day, any day, any year, is a new day – a brand new, never before seen day, a day to renew efforts to make our lives and the lives of those around us better.

It's a time for each of us to do six things:

1. Refuse to be shackled or hampered by yesterday's failures.
2. What we don't know will no longer be a problem – it'll be an opportunity, a challenge, to learn and to grow.
3. Refuse to allow others to define our mood, method, image or mission – if they've been mean or said bad things about you, it's a chance to do what Jesus did for all of us – to forgive.
4. Let's make our mission greater than ourselves by making at least one person happy that he or she saw us.
5. Don't make time for self-pity, gossip or negative thoughts – from ourselves or from others.
6. Be thankful for all our blessings – large and small. Be thankful for the comfort, strength, courage, and insight or direction that God gives each of us to confront troubles or problems. And thank God that we can call on Jesus and the Holy Spirit to help us learn and grow as we face each new day.

And what about tomorrow? It's another new day!

Fugle's note: I honestly don't remember if I wrote this originally or if I read it somewhere. While researching for what I hoped would become a book, I came across this in my files of past articles. I think I used it in a church newsletter years ago and perhaps as one of my columns in past years.

At any rate, the six points appear to be good goals to aim for. Probably no one will ever achieve 100 percent success. But we can try again and again to do better. After all each day is a new day.

Have a happy – and better – new year.

Watch those words

As a writer, I work with words.

Some people say there's magic in words. Maybe. But I think it's more than magic. There is power in words – awesome power, for better or worse, good or bad. Think about it.

Without words, I'd be out of business and the world would be out of languages. We'd somehow communicate by grunts and groans, squawks and squeaks, shrugs and nods, mumbles and moans. Come to think of it, occasionally I've been accused of that myself.

But seriously, on the down side, words can incite, inflame, insult, injure, irritate, irk. They can tear down, undermine, destroy, slander, smear, ruin, gossip, swear, condemn, complain, convey hate, and lie.

Fortunately, words also have an up side. They can praise, compliment, soothe, calm, encourage, help, explain, entertain, amuse, stimulate, forgive, cheer, convey hope, teach, communicate, clarify, create images, assure, and say, "I love you."

Without words how would writers write, poets compose, attorneys argue, singers sing, rappers rap, preachers preach? How would cheerleaders lead, cheerers cheer, politicians promise, salesmen sell, exhorters exhort, naggers nag, teachers teach, and greeters greet? What would libraries lend?

As Mayor Shin in *The Music Man* liked to tell his wife, "Eulalie, watch your phraseology!"

The *real* Easter

Stuffed animals, live chicks, decorated eggs, chocolate-covered marshmallow bunnies, new spring apparel, style shows, fashion parades, egg hunts, spring breaks, short vacations, ham dinners and snapshots of the kids in all their new Easter season finery. That's all OK – if kept in perspective.

But let's remember the real Easter -- because Easter without Jesus is like Christmas without Christ.

The last supper, prayers in Gethsemane, the betrayal and arrest of Jesus, the mock trial, a cock crowing three times as Peter denied any connection with his Lord, the scourging, a crown of thorns, suffering, anguish, despair, the march to Calvary, Christ's plea for forgiveness for his tormentors, the sacrifice, and death on the cross, burial in a garden tomb.

But then on the third day came the joyous promise of Easter. The resurrection! A stone rolled away, an empty tomb, encounters with the risen Lord on the Emmaus Road, His appearance among the apostles in the upper room, convincing the doubting Thomas that it was Jesus standing before him.

Gifts from God: Forgiveness, salvation, an incomprehensible love, promise of joy and eternal life.

Such is the real Easter.

Could it happen again?

Just finished reading *Darkest Before Dawn: Sedition and Free Speech in the American West* by UM journalism Professor Clem Work.

Much of it details pertains to fanatical reactions to perceived seditious statements made by people during World War I. Sedition is defined as the illegal promotion of resistance against the government, usually in speech or writing.

The Montana sedition law was enacted by a special session of the Legislature in February 1918. It criminalized just about anything negative that was said or written about the government in time of war. The maximum penalty was 20 years in prison and a $20,000 fine.

Particularly at risk of prosecution were folks of German ancestry. Also under fire were German language church services, school courses in German language, and even textbooks with references to Germany were burned.

A total of 74 persons were convicted of sedition during 1918-1919 under what Work termed "perhaps the harshest anti-speech law ever passed by any state in the history of the United States."

Work explained that most of the people convicted under the Montana sedition law "worked at menial blue collar or rural jobs. Half were farmers, ranchers, laborers and some were convicted on witness accounts of casual statements, which were often made in saloons."

Hardly an organized spy ring or group designed to overthrow the government despite how rancorous some may have sounded as they vented their frustrations.

Could it happen again in America?

Fortunately, freedom of speech and press are more closely protected today.

But over the years I've learned never to take anything for granted. There are so many hot trigger issues that raise emotional levels today – Iraq, Iran, Afghanistan, abortion vs. pro-life, swine flu, unemployment, politics, the environment, subdivisions, zoning, even the Wal-Mart controversy.

In such emotional issues it's important that the people involved keep things in perspective. Listen respectfully to both sides, avoid hearsay and gossip, and focus on the issues.

After decisions are finally made, probably no one will be completely happy. But we all have to live together peacefully, respectfully and responsibly.

Why write?

A few years ago when I was trying my hand at freelance writing, I was visiting with a lady seated next to me on a flight between Salt Lake City and Missoula. Conversation led around to asking what sort of work I was involved in. I told her I did a bit of freelance writing.

"Oh? Why do you write?" she asked.

I wished she had asked what I wrote, not why.

That would have been easier to answer: Travel pieces, profiles, business articles, faith or inspirational stories, humor, columns, history, even some stabs at short fiction.

But why?

I gave an off the cuff, flip answer and that was the end of the conversation. But it did get me to thinking about really why I like to write. Perhaps to earn money should be a top reason but it isn't – there are thousands of easier ways to earn money than freelance writing. Among other reasons for writing, though, are the challenge of it, the chance to help bring recognition to folks for their achievements, the opportunity to share joys and sorrows, triumphs and tragedies; accomplishments and frustrations; those are the slices of everyday life.

Inspirational stories can affect readers by making them feel something – to laugh, cry, care, appreciate, sympathize, emphasize, to find or re-discover hope, motivation and sense of purpose.

Looking for new angles and new information about old topics can make history an adventure. And there's a possibility that business profiles or new product stories can help create new jobs.

Writers usually feel the people they write about have something to say, something to offer. And ego plays a role, too. Garrison Keillor says that "shy people" write so that folks will notice them.

I suppose we do, otherwise we'd be among billions of faceless specks on this planet because we feel we really don't do many things well enough to gain attention.

Anyway, a final word of advice: If you ever find yourself on an airplane seated next to someone who fancies himself or herself a writer, just ask what they write, not why. It's a heckuva lot easier to answer.

Time's a wasting

I've always wondered why there just doesn't seem to be enough hours in the day to get things accomplished. Now I know. In my brother Norman Wright's book, *Simplify Your Life*, he quotes time analysts whose studies have shown that in the "average" life span, a person will have 1,086 "sick days"; spend eight months opening junk mail; spend two years on the telephone; wait in line for five years, and wait in traffic for nine months.

Norm writes, "Just the basic necessities of life consume a large quantity of time. You'll spend four years cooking and eating (you can't live on McDonald's, Burger King, and Taco Bell all the time. If you do, you may have part of the reason for the 1,086 sick days). You'll spend a year and a half dressing, a year and a half grooming, and seven years in bathrooms! Finally, the time experts tell us we'll spend twenty-four years sleeping and three years shopping."

He describes the "time bank" that everyone has, citing Leslie Flynn's book *It's about Time:* "It's called the First World Bank of Time. Each morning the bank credits your account with 86,400 seconds. That's the same as 1,440 minutes or 24 hours. It's the same for each one of us. And keep in mind that no balance is carried over the next day. If you choose not to use it, you lose it. You can't accumulate it."

As a professional procrastinator, my motto has been "Never do today what can be put off until tomorrow." One of these days, I'm gonna have to change my ways.

The Writer's Prayer

Lord, give me an insight and sensitivity to people and events around me that I might always have an abundance of stories to write.

Give me the ability to write wisely and well, to write in a way that will enrich and enlighten the hearts and minds of others.

Give me the courage to write clean and true, regardless of what others around me may be writing.

Help me to remember always that words have the power to destroy – or build; the power to spread ignorance – or dispense knowledge; the power to darken the world with hate – or light it with love.

Help me to continue writing through those black moments of discouragement when I feel that nothing I write is good or worthwhile or will ever be read by anyone.

And Lord, daily help me to have faith in my writing and in myself, even though no one else may have faith in either.

In Jesus' name,

Amen

Author unknown -- I keep this posted above my desk and try to use it as a daily guideline in writing.

Sundown along the trail

June 1961 marked the 43rd year that the owners of the Melton ranch, 10 miles west of Sloan's Bridge, near Ronan, Montana, had trail-driven their cattle over a three-day stretch to summer grazing land near Lake Mary Ronan.

The first day found the trail herd going along the west side of the Flathead River to the Buffalo Ferry Bridge site, where camp was set up, and supper was prepared by Mrs. Neal Melton and Mrs. Ike Melton.

I happened to drive by the campsite shortly after a thunder shower had rumbled through the area. The two silhouetted cowboys were watching the cattle settling down just over the ridge. The sunset in the west afforded a memorable western scene, which resulted in my favorite photo.

The next day the herd was trailed through Irvine Flats, up the hill, past Loon Lake and down to Highway 93. From there the critters were trailed along the side of the highway to about two miles south of Elmo where camp was set up again and Ike Melton took over the cooking chores.

On the third day, the herd proceeded along Highway 93, past Chief Cliff and then inland to the Lake Mary Ronan area for summer grazing. In the fall, the cattle were trailed back over the route to the home ranch.

Short Stories
(Fiction)

Black sheep

To a ten-year-old, phrases like "family black sheep" and "a skeleton in the closet" have a visual connotation. My mother's Aunt Dorothy fit this category.

Although I had never met her, I knew exactly how she'd look -- a tall, stern, humorless, thin woman wearing a black wool coat. With this unhappy image in mind, I sat beside Mother as she drove the family '36 Chevy to Lockheed Air Terminal in Burbank, Calif., that warm day in December 1940. Aunt Dorothy had telegraphed from Montana that she would arrive on the Trans-Western afternoon flight.

Just as we entered the terminal Mother was paged by a gravelly-voiced man asking her to report to the Trans-Western counter. There the ticket agent handed her a telegram: "Not on airliner. Arriving hour later, different plane. Dorothy."

I was crushed. I had hoped that we could go out on the parking apron and greet her getting off the plane. I fantasized that Aunt Dorothy would forget her coat and purse and ask me to retrieve them from inside that shiny, silver, Douglas DC-3. Then the pilot would invite me to inspect the cockpit -- even sit in his place.

He'd say, "Here, son, check out this yoke. I thought it felt a little mushy. What do you think?" And I'd chomp on my chewing gym, push and pull on the wheel, and finally look at him confidently and answer, "Naw, it's OK."

Now it would never happen.

"It's all your Aunt Dorothy's fault," I blurted, half-sobbing.

"What is?"

"Oh, nothing. Never mind."

Right on time, the 14-passenger DC-3 that should have carried Aunt Dorothy taxied up and stopped outside the terminal. The plane's door opened, steps folded down, and a beautiful, smiling, uniformed angel descended to bid farewell to the departing passengers. I was one glum kid -- staring through the plate glass window in the hot, stuffy waiting room. It just wasn't fair.

Mother told me, "Oh, come on cheer up. No doubt we're in for a surprise. We never know what to expect from Aunt Dorothy." Her voice sounded odd. The tone seemed to be a blend of uncertainty, apprehension, and envy.

"Are there any other flights arriving this afternoon," she asked the agent.

'No, Ma'am. Next flight is due at six tonight."

Mother's brow furrowed, as it always did when she was perplexed. She mumbled, "What next?" Displeasure was evident.

About fifteen minutes before the hour was up, she said, "Let's go outside and wait by the fence. We can see her plane from there. It's cooler there, too."

Neither of us knew what kind of airplane to look for. Several small planes took off and landed, but none taxied near the terminal. Then we noticed -- heard, actually -- the loudest racket of the afternoon as a low-flying, single engine biplane passed over the edge of the field. The noise was like a thousand exploding Fourth of July firecrackers -- the kind all the other kids could have, but I couldn't.

A man standing nearby remarked, "Hey, that's an old Eagle Rock. I wonder where it came from."

We watched the Eagle Rock land and clatter toward the terminal where it stopped in a tie-down area near the fence. As the pilot shut down the motor we heard a piercing, "Yee-haw, hi there!"

I glanced at Mother. Her face was pale. She clasped her hands to her stomach and moaned, "Oh, no. I should have known. That's Aunt Dorothy."

I looked back at the plane. The pilot, a bear of a man, was climbing out of the rear cockpit. I stared, wide-eyed. What a contrast to the spiffy airline crew. This pilot had a black, bushy beard, strands of hair dangling beneath the edge of his leather helmet. He wore greasy, once-white coveralls.

The plane was an equal mess: Red patches on the yellow fabric wings; a big blue splotch on the dirty, yellow left stabilizer; faded, crude lettering on the green fuselage, "Big Bob's Flying Circus."

"Well, don't just stand there, Bob. Help me down," Aunt Dorothy ordered in a sharp, high-pitched voice.

"Yes, Ma'am," the burly pilot growled.

Then, more disillusionment. As she emerged from the cockpit, backside first, Aunt Dorothy was far from the image in my mind. She wore a brown leather jacket, floppy brown slacks, and brown shoes. She left her helmet in the plane but her ruddy face bore the telltale marks of too-tight goggles. Even her still-flattened, close-cropped, iron-gray hair was the wrong color. Short and squat, she reminded me of a barrel with shoes as she climbed down, steadied by Bob.

The pilot fished a suitcase from the front cockpit and a medium-sized box from behind the rear seat, and set them on the ground. Aunt Dorothy took an envelope from her jacket pocket, handed it to the pilot and said crisply, "I'll keep the jacket as a souvenir, Bob, here's your owner's certificate. I'll handle the freight."

She slapped him hard on the shoulder, and said sharply, "There's enough money in the envelope to refuel and get to that San Diego air show. But for Pete's sake, Bob, get a haircut, have that beard trimmed, and buy a clean pair of coveralls. Then get a decent paint job on that plane."

Her voice lowered slightly as she told him, "And, Bob, have merry Christmas. Now go. Shoo! Scat! Scram!"

Suddenly Bob perked up. A broad, toothy grin beamed from the brush-covered face. His brown eyes seemed to glisten.

"Yes, Ma'am, I'll do that. And thanks. Merry Christmas to you, too." His voice sounded like he'd swallowed his gum or something, like he was choking. But he seemed to spring into the cockpit. He quickly started the noisy engine and taxied over to the gas pumps.

Aunt Dorothy picked up her gear and headed toward the terminal door. "Meet me inside," she called to us.

As I was introduced, I meekly responded, "Hello, Ant Dorothy." She guffawed, "Oh, come on, Buster, that's *Aunt* Dorothy -- with a broad A, just like mine." I blushed as she slapped her posterior and added, "Remember: ants crawl, aunts don't."

On the drive home, pieces of the puzzle began to fit together as Aunt Dorothy explained to us the reason for her surprise visit. She had been teaching high school English in a small town north of Great Falls, but the school board disapproved of one of her extracurricular activities -- motorcycling. That fall, board members told her that riding to and from school -- and everywhere else -- on her Harley-Davidson was "unbecoming to a woman teacher."

"Unbecoming my foot," she said, "I didn't violate any dress rules. I kept my classroom clothes at school and changed from coveralls and back again before and after school."

After she refused to comply with the demands, the board simply told her not to return after the holidays. That was fine with me. I told them that a person can't live with lifelong adventure without becoming addicted to it."

She told us that she had put in too many years kayaking, mushing dog sleds, snow-shoeing, and coping with the challenges of living and teaching in the Aleutians and the Alaskan territorial interior. Why, she had even cooked for Canadian loggers and Montana hunting guides.

Her tone softened, "In the last two years, I've realized that I can't do some of the things I did ten or fifteen years ago. I accept that. But riding that Harley at age 63 was something I could do, and I needed that to keep my perspective."

My ten-year-old brain understood. I wondered why those grown-up school board members couldn't.

The spark returned to her voice: "They told me teachers had to be more 'ladylike;' that I wasn't living on the frontier anymore. One even said I was living in the past.

"I replied, 'You're wrong. I *am* living on the frontier -- because every new day is a frontier. No, I'm not living in the past. I'm just living a few decades ahead. Just wait, you'll see.'"

Because it was impractical for her to ride the motorcycle to California in the winter, she sold it, intending to buy an airplane ticket. However, a blizzard caused cancellation of all flights to and from Great Falls, and she spent the night in the airport's small waiting room. There she joined some stranded male passengers and the barnstorming Bob in a poker game.

"I won $328 more from Bob than he had on him. I insisted that he give me title to his airplane. Then I handed him $100 and ordered him to fly me to Burbank when the weather cleared."

"Why didn't you keep the airplane and learn to fly it?" I asked.

"Because that pilot needed to learn a couple of lessons: 1. Never gamble more than you can afford to lose; 2. Don't play poker with a strange woman -- especially one who learned the game from north woods lumberjacks. Besides, I'd already flown, and I was ready for a new experience.

"Oh, by the way, I leave the day after Christmas. I'm joining two retired teachers on a trip around the world on a tramp steamer. That's something I've never done."

She added "Also, I wanted to give that barnstormer something for Christmas that he'd never forget."

Aunt Dorothy's presence that Christmas gave us all something special to remember. Dad drove her to the pier at San Pedro on December 26th. Mother and I went along and bade her bon voyage. We never saw her again.

In late February local newspapers carried a brief wire service bulletin: "The tramp steamer *Black Sheep* broke apart and sank in a storm yesterday off the Philippines. All aboard were lost -- including a trio of retired American school teachers."

One more hill to home

It was Christmas Eve, one of those crystal clear, sharp, snapping cold, zero degree winter nights common to the northern Rockies. A myriad of glittering pinpoints punctuated the black skies. Starshine combined with light from a last quarter moon to cast an eerie glow over the snowscape as silver smoke ribbons curled upward from ranch house chimneys.

Along the straight stretch of two-lane highway purred a miles-weary '41 Chevy. Inside the car, the heater waged a losing battle against the invisible force of bone-chilling cold that penetrated the four-door sedan's metal skin.

Jim Creighton hunkered his 6'2" frame deeper inside his fleece-lined parka trying to find an extra degree of warmth.

"Only one more hill to home," he mused. "It's been a long time and a long way."

A couple of days earlier he had received his final Army discharge papers. And a couple of months before that he had been half-a world away on a bald, shell-pocked, nameless numbered hill in South Korea, where he wondered he'd ever see another Christmas, let alone be home for the holiday.

Over the car radio he heard a medley of Christmas carols. Jim joined in, humming at first, and then tentatively singing the melody. Realizing no one could hear him, he tried harmonizing to the more familiar carols.

"Bah, I harmonize about like McGuffey's goat. No wonder the teachers told me just to keep quiet and mouth the words during grade school music times."

Traffic, never heavy in the sparsely populated Montana foothills, was virtually non-existent. He'd met only two cars in the last ten miles and no lights showed in the rearview mirror.

"All right, just another hour and I'll be home," Jim thought as he and the old Chevy started climbing the twisting mountain road toward Windy Pass. About a third of the way up, he noticed the quarter moon and stars had disappeared. A few light flakes of snow reflecting in the headlights grabbed his attention.

"Should have expected this," he said aloud. "Seems like there's always weather on Windy Pass. Even in the summer it's wet here when the whole state is dry."

Christmas Eve was no exception. The flakes rapidly turned into a full scale snowstorm. He dimmed the high beam to better concentrate on the snow-covered road. After a few miles of steady climbing, he noticed the speedometer racing to 50 miles an hour as the wheels slipped and spun on the ice beneath the snow blanket.

The combination of slipping wheels, rolled up windows and relentless oncoming snowflakes literally hypnotized Jim, producing a disoriented feeling. He rolled down the window on the driver's side and switched on the interior light. The trance-like feeling subsided, but the windblown snow stung his face. He rolled the window up again as car and driver approached a pullout three miles below the summit.

Jim had noted during the past mile that the snow had started to drift across the highway and the car plowed through with increasing difficulty.

"No wonder there isn't any traffic out here tonight. Just three miles to the top though. If I can get over that, the going should be easier on the east side," he thought, "but I'm going to chain up to get to the top."

He pulled over at the turnoff, stopped, got the chains out of the trunk, fumbled first with gloves, then without, as he managed to fasten the chains around the rear wheels.

"Wonder how much more snow has accumulated in just fifteen minutes," he pondered as the Chevy resumed its snow-clogged climb. Even with chains it was difficult going the last three miles to the top.

"At least in Korea when I heard shells coming I could duck or dig in; but here I'm really exposed. There's nowhere to hide. Lord, please help me," he prayed.

The innovative combination of the overhead light, low beams, a slightly cracked window and steadily shifting glances seemed to work, yet Jim was exhausted when the car reached the summit and started down the eastern slope. However, the expected respite from the storm failed to materialize. The wind had died down but the heavy snowfall continued.

"I'd better be thankful for little things," he told himself. "At least we're over the top and heading downhill. This can't get any worse."

The euphoric feeling didn't last long. Suddenly, near the bottom of the hill, Jim ducked as a brown-gray object caromed off the hood and into the windshield. As he instinctively raised an arm to protect his face, he jerked the steering wheel just enough to throw the car into an uncontrollable slide. After a couple 360s, it went into a 30-ft. deep borrow pit, and overturned twice. As the car tumbled, Jim cried aloud, "Please, God, stop this thing…"

Somehow the doors remained shut and the car came to a stop, upside down at the bottom of the borrow pit. All was quiet as the snow continued to fall.

In a matter of minutes Jim stirred, blinked blurry eyes and gradually regained consciousness. He figured he must have banged his head as the car rolled. Gingerly he moved his arms and legs. He reached out – and felt feathers.

"Feathers? What on earth … ?" Little more than a foot away was a dead owl. It had flown toward the Chevy's headlights and paid the price.

As Jim became more alert he heard singing – "O, come all ye faithful, joyful and triumphant …' He thought the radio must still be playing. Then he realized it wasn't; it was too badly damaged.

Unable to force the doors open, he cleared off the remaining parts of the windshield and squeezed through. Once outside, he realized the snow had stopped. He still heard the singing – "O' little town of Bethlehem, how still we see thee lie…"

Minutes before, a rousing round of "Deck the halls with boughs of holly" had drowned out the sound of the crash. Those in the Foothills Community Church were unaware of Jim Creighton's encounter with the stray owl, barely 50 yards away.

He made his way through the snow to the church and opened the door, walked slowly in and knelt gratefully as the service was closing with the singing of "Silent night, holy night, all is calm…"

Thirty-three years later on Christmas Eve, Jim and Jennie had finished dinner and were relaxing in front of the fireplace before getting ready to attend the community Christmas Eve candlelight service. On the mantel were photographs of their five kids – each now grown and living elsewhere, three in Montana and two out of state. Christmases were a lot quieter now.

Jennie looked at her husband and commented, "Jim, you're looking pretty pensive. What are you thinking?"

"Oh, about that Christmas Eve thirty-three years ago tonight. I'm glad that Foothills church was still there. Two days later it wasn't."

An electrical short circuit started a fire the day after Christmas and the building burned to the ground. It never was rebuilt – better cars, improved roads, found folks traveling to town to attend church.

Jennie's eyes misted as she smiled, took his hand and said softly, "Mmmm. I sang in the choir that night. I still cringe when I think that I almost decided not to go to that Christmas Eve service. I'm glad I did."

"Me, too."